# The
# MIDLAND & SOUTH WESTERN JUNCTION RAILWAY

by
T.B. Sands
(Revised by S.C. Jenkins, BA, Cert Ed, MA)

## THE OAKWOOD PRESS

© Oakwood Press 1990

First Edition 1959
Reprinted 1975 and 1979
Second Revised Edition 1990

ISBN 0 85361 402 4


Typeset by Gem Publishing Company, Brightwell, Wallingford, Oxfordshire.

Printed by Alpha Print, Witney, Oxford.

An idyllic view of Cricklade station looking south towards Andover Junction on 12th August, 1955.                                                                    *H.B. Priestley*

Published by
The OAKWOOD PRESS
P.O.Box 122, Headington, Oxford.

# Contents

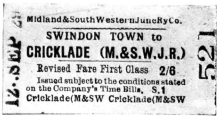

3

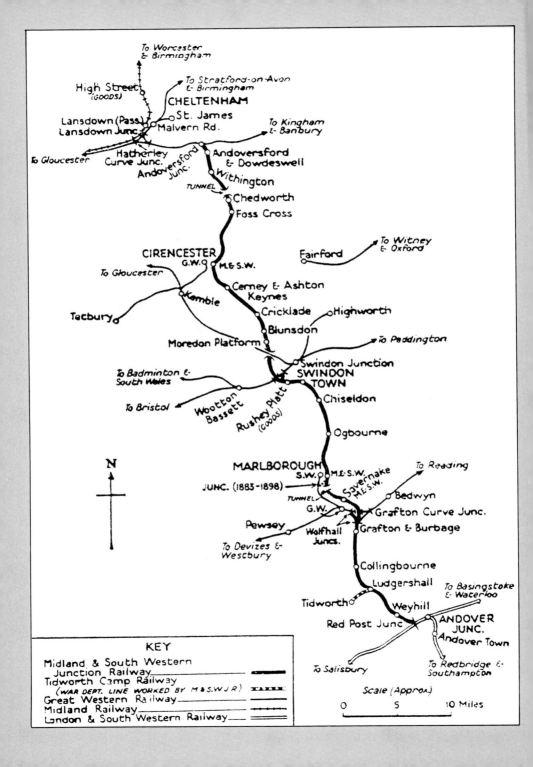

# Introduction

The Midland & South Western Junction Railway has been the subject of at least three books, but this history by the late T.B. Sands — first published in 1959 — was the very first to appear. The original text was, in many ways, a minor classic which epitomised all that was best in the Oakwood Library of Railway History; solidly based upon original sources, it avoided most of the pitfalls that have come to afflict some present day 'branch line' histories. There was, for example, no attempt to present the reader with an endless succession of meaningless quotes — instead the author wove a clever synthesis from his study of minute books, Acts and contemporary documents, the result being a concise but readable account of this interesting minor railway.

Although *The Midland & South Western Junction Railway* was reprinted in 1975 and again in 1979, the book has remained a much-sought after title, and it was felt appropriate that the work should now be republished in a modern format. In this new edition, the text has been sub-divided into five chapters, and while the narrative incorporates most of the old text, a much-expanded 'route' chapter has been included. There is now a brief descriptive section relating to each station, together with a selection of photographs for each location.

In general, the new text remains true to the author's original conception, but at the same time an opportunity has been taken to clarify certain points and add new information where appropriate. It should be stressed, however, that the 1959 version *was* a definitive work, and in revising and expanding the original text I have tried not to impose my own style or idioms — *The Midland & South Western Junction Railway* deserves to reach a new generation of readers in an expanded, but little altered form.

This new version of *The Midland & South Western Junction Railway* is, therefore, an enlarged and updated version of the T.B. Sands classic with a new route section and many new photographs; it is hoped that T.B. Sands would have approved of the transformation, and that if he had lived long enough to rewrite his own book, he would have produced something not so very different from the present volume.

*Stanley C. Jenkins*
March 1990                                       *Witney, Oxfordshire*

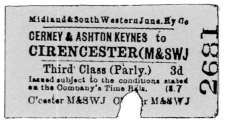

MSWJ 4 – 4 – 0 locomotive No. 1 leaves Cheltenham Lansdown station with a down train.

R.W. Kidner

# Chapter One

## Origins and Opening (1846–1891)

One of the problems that frequently vexed the Great Western Railway was that of repelling north-to-south invasions of its territory by competitive companies, to which it was very vulnerable, especially while it retained the distinctive broad gauge. In 1845 the line from Bristol to Gloucester was snapped up by the Midland Railway, and thereafter it was the accepted policy of the GWR to oppose or seek to control any north-to-south project which appeared at all threatening; yet despite its vigilance, three through routes at length came into being astride its territory, and two of them eluded its grasp.

The most easterly, the Didcot, Newbury & Southampton Railway, had little chance of freedom; although nominally independent for some fifty years (1873–1923), it dragged out in practice an impoverished existence as a helpless prisoner of the Great Western. The most westerly, the Somerset & Dorset Railway, which the GWR had thought to have well within its grip, escaped into rival hands and was leased jointly to the London & South Western and Midland companies in 1875. The middle line of the trio, the Midland & South Western Junction Railway, achieved in the face of great adversity a degree of real and triumphant independence which it retained, with the help of two powerful allies, until in 1923 it was thrust willy-nilly into the fold of its traditional enemy.

### Early Schemes

Proposals for a railway running southwards from Cheltenham to the coast through Gloucestershire, Wiltshire and Hampshire date back to the years of the Railway Mania. In the summer of 1846, at the height of the Mania, a Bill was before Parliament to incorporate the Manchester & Southampton Railway, with power to make a railway commencing by a junction with the Birmingham & Gloucester line of the Midland Railway near the 44th milepost from Birmingham (about 1½ miles north of Cheltenham) and terminating in Bugle Street, Southampton, near the entrance to the Royal Pier.

The course proposed for this line of 88 miles 36 chains, as planned by Robert Stephenson (1803–59) and G.P. Bidder (1806–78), ran through the Cotswolds via Cirencester into the Vale of White Horse at Cricklade; from there it passed to the east of Swindon, climbed through the Marlborough Downs, and crossed the valley of the River Kennet at Marlborough. Finally, after skirting Savernake Forest and the fringes of Salisbury Plain, it reached the River Test, leading down to Southampton, south of Andover.

The plans included gradients of 1 in 75 and a tunnel 2961 yds long on the climb out of Cheltenham into the valley of the River Churn north of Cirencester, together with a viaduct 306 yds long with a maximum height of 46 feet at Marlborough, and further tunnels totalling 2514 yds through the high ground bordering on Savernake Forest. In all there would have been about four miles of tunnel.

It was not claimed that local traffic alone would ever justify the capital cost of such a railway, estimated at £1,500,000, towards which the Midland had agreed to contribute £400,000. The object of the promoters, as the title 'Manchester & Southampton' implied, was to forge a standard-gauge link across the belt of territory occupied by the broad gauge (7 ft) line of the Great Western from London to Bristol, so that traffic could pass north and south without break of gauge.

A rival project, the Manchester, Southampton & Poole Railway, took a somewhat similar course north of Marlborough but proceeded thence via Pewsey, Durrington, and Porton to a junction at Salisbury with an authorised branch of the London & South Western Railway from Bishopstoke (Eastleigh) on the London to Southampton main line. The Manchester, Southampton & Poole line was then to continue southwards through Fordingbridge to a junction with the Southampton and Dorchester line about three miles west of Ringwood. This scheme, promoted by Charles Henry Lacy of Kenyon House, near Manchester, with Joseph Locke (1805–60) as its Engineer, made little progress in Parliament.

The Manchester & Southampton promoters, however, came very near to success. Despite intense opposition from the GWR and from several landowners, their Bill passed the House of Commons, only to suffer defeat by the narrow margin of the Chairman's casting vote in the House of Lords Committee after the Great Western had given a pledge to lay the mixed gauge between Oxford and Basingstoke. A Bill for a modified version of the Manchester & Southampton scheme was brought forward in 1847, but this new proposal was even less successful than its abortive predecessor, and failed at an early stage.

### Isolation in Central Wiltshire

Nevertheless, the through route thus created (when the GWR pledge was at length honoured in 1856) was rather circuitous and did nothing to ease the lack of communications in central Wiltshire, where journeys between north and south in the middle of last century were fraught with difficulty.

The town of Marlborough in particular felt its isolation very keenly; generations of boys, seeking to reach its famous public school from the Swindon direction, had to face a journey of acute discomfort across the Marlborough Downs in a noisome, horse-drawn vehicle known as 'Jerry 'Ammond's Bus'. A.G. Bradley, author of *Round about Wiltshire*, who was at Marlborough from 1862 to 1867, has described in his history of the school:

> . . . the rigours of the coach-roof on a winter's dawn when a north wind blew over that wild chalk plateau between Halfway House and Ogbourne . . . the amazing contempt for time that marked the getting under way in the darkness of that rattling chariot, which, between the decay of coaching and the extension of the railroad, formed the chief connecting link between Marlborough and Swindon Station; the musty smell of the straw-littered floor and time-worn velvet seats.

A tempting field thus lay open for local enterprise and speculative promoters, whose efforts continued to trouble the Great Western for many years. None of the more grandiose schemes came to anything, but by 1870 some portions of the route mapped out for the Manchester & Southampton line had been filled, notably the section south of Andover, which had been occupied by the Andover & Redbridge Railway, incorporated on 12th July, 1858. The Andover & Redbridge was acquired by the London & South Western Railway in 1863, and after a chequered career — including an unsuccessful attempt to extend northwards to join the Berks & Hants Extension Railway at Savernake — the A&RR was opened throughout from Andover Junction to Redbridge Junction on 6th March, 1865. (The Berks & Hants Extension was opened on 11th November, 1862 and worked by the Great Western as a broad gauge single line; it was fully absorbed by the GWR in 1882.)

Beyond Savernake station on the Berks & Hants Extension lay the only feasible route which a railway, aspiring to press on northwards, could take over the high, undulating plateau separating the Vale of Pewsey from the Kennet valley at Marlborough. This strategic gap was secured by the Great Western, when it undertook to lease and work a 5½ mile broad gauge branch from Savernake to Marlborough; the branch was authorised by the Marlborough Railway Act of 22nd July, 1861, and it opened to public traffic on 14th April, 1864.

The new branch was severely graded, with a section of 1 in 61 at the Savernake end, and over a mile of 1 in 58 near the terminus at Marlborough. (The line remained broad gauge until 1874 when, with other GWR lines in the area, it was converted to standard gauge.)

## The Swindon Marlborough & Andover Railway

Although the Marlborough branch provided useful transport facilities for the surrounding area, many local people still hoped that one day their town could be placed on a main line, and on 25th May, 1872 a group of prominent citizens from Marlborough and Swindon met in the Forest Hotel at Savernake to consider some plans laid before them by John Sewell, a London engineer. It was suggested that a 'Swindon Marlborough Southampton & New Forest Railway' might be built in three stages, namely Swindon to Marlborough, Marlborough to Andover, and Andover to the Solent via Fawley. These proposals were of great interest to the landowners and tradesmen of north-eastern Wiltshire, and in an atmosphere of unbounded enthusiasm the promoters decided to form a company in order that the suggested rail link could be built.

The title adopted in a subsequent prospectus was the 'Swindon Marlborough & Andover Railway', and a Bill seeking to incorporate a company of that name, with a capital of £375,000 and borrowing powers of £125,000, was tabled for the 1873 session of Parliament.

The Swindon Marlborough & Andover promoters experienced some difficulty in raising the necessary Parliamentary deposit, and indeed the chances of such a line ever being built in its entirety seemed so slight that nobody found it worth while to press opposition very far. Thus, the Bill had an easy passage, and on 21st July, 1873 the Swindon Marlborough & Andover Railway Act (36 & 37 Vic. cap. 194) received the Royal Assent.

The Swindon Marlborough & Andover Route, as authorised in 1873, comprised separate northern and southern sections, connecting with the intervening Marlborough branch. The northern section was to start on a curve of 13 chains radius, immediately to the east of Swindon station on the Great Western Railway main line from London to Bristol, and terminate at Marlborough by an end-on junction with the branch from Savernake, involving a tunnel 773 yds long at Swindon and an embankment or viaduct at Marlborough with a maximum height of 67 feet.

The deposited plans contemplated the doubling and regrading of the Marlborough Railway onwards to Savernake, with a ruling gradient of 1 in 90 instead of 1 in 58, and similar improvements on the Berks & Hants Extension Railway for 60 chains eastward from Savernake station to the commencement of the southern section near Wolfhall Bridge. However, the Act itself confined the Swindon Marlborough & Andover Railway to the making of junctions with those railways, while granting running powers over the Marlborough Railway between Marlborough and Wolfhall.

The southern section was defined as a railway commencing at Wolfhall Junction and terminating near milepost 67¾ on the London & South Western main line, about one and a half miles west of Andover Junction station. An agreement scheduled to the Swindon Marlborough & Andover Act provided that there would be no physical connection with the L&SWR at the point of convergence, and instead, a third line would be laid from 'the Abbotts Ann Junction' to Andover Junction station. This third line would be the property of the London & South Western Railway, but the line would be leased to the Swindon Marlborough & Andover company at 5 per cent per annum on the cost of the works (i.e. £23,141).

It is interesting to note that Abbotts Ann Junction — derived from the name of the parish in which it was situated — was being called Red Posts or Red Post by 1879 (if not earlier) and the junction was known as Red Post Junction for most of its life. (Land needed for the widening was purchased by the SM&A and did not pass into L&SWR ownership until 1912, when it was conveyed free of charge under the terms of the 1873 agreement.)

## Construction Begins

In its early days, the Swindon Marlborough & Andover Railway was able to procure some wide publicity but very little cash. *The Illustrated London News* depicted Lord Ernest Brudenell-Bruce, MP for Marlborough and first Chairman of the company, with a large gathering of notables, performing the ceremony of turning the first sod on 28th July, 1875, off Coldharbour Lane, Marlborough, on a site earmarked for a proposed 'joint' station north-east of the town centre, though by that date less than £6000 had been subscribed towards the estimated capital cost of £400,000. Nevertheless, despite the shortage of money (and an ill-omened collapse of the ceremonial barrow at the climax of the inaugural function), a contract was let for the construction of the whole line, and work started in Belle Vue, Swindon, on the northern approach to the proposed tunnel.

Sadly, the contractor quickly proved to be a man of straw; his tunnel works showed a disconcerting tendency to cave in, and although the company proceeded with them on its own account, and even laid a few rails, funds ran out and everything came to a standstill in October 1876. (Later buildings and the creation of the Queen's Gardens in Belle Vue have obscured any obvious trace of this early work in Swindon, though it may be significant that there is a gap in the line of houses on the north side of Hunt Street, near the junction with Victoria Road, where it would seem from the plans that the line would have entered the tunnel.)

The whole enterprise then lay moribund until 1878, when a marked fall in the cost of labour, capital, and materials, and some slight evidence of support from Southampton shipowners, brought hopes of revival for the Swindon Marlborough & Andover when it was on the verge of abandonment. Indeed, the company was kept alive during those critical years only by the efforts and determination of its solicitor, J.C. Townsend, of Swindon, and of one or two local Directors, notably the Rev. J.S. Thomas, bursar of Marlborough College.

In September 1879, Messrs Watson, Smith & Watson undertook the construction of the whole railway on terms guaranteeing interest payments to shareholders at 5 per cent per annum until the line was open for traffic, and three successive Acts — 16th July, 1878 (extension of time), 3rd July, 1879 (deviations), and 29th June, 1880 (power to pay preference dividends) — paved the way for the scheme to go forward.

The deviations authorised by the Act of 1879 were designed to reduce cost by eliminating some of the more expensive structures on the northern section, at the price of a ruling gradient of 1 in 75 instead of 1 in 100. At Swindon, a tunnel was avoided by taking the railway round the west side of the hill on which the old town stands from a junction with the GWR at Rushey Platt, while curves and embankments replaced proposed viaducts at Chiseldon and Marlborough. The wide curve needed to the east of Marlborough had the incidental effect of bringing the Swindon Marlborough & Andover line into contact with the Great Western branch from Savernake at a point some 25 chains short of the GWR terminus, with the result that the SM&A company had to build a separate station barely 200 yds from the Great Western terminal. This Swindon Marlborough & Andover station was situated on a low level site to the east of its Great Western counterpart, and separated from it by an intervening main road.

Construction of the northern section between Swindon and Marlborough went ahead rapidly, and 11¼ miles of single line were formally opened on 26th July, 1881. Public services commenced on the following day, when local trains began running between Marlborough and the Swindon Marlborough & Andover station in Swindon old town. There were intermediate stations at Chiseldon and Ogbourne, and both stations had crossing loops — although only one platform was initially provided at these wayside stopping places.

## Great Western Opposition

A long struggle ensued before the isolated Marlborough to Swindon line could be linked for public traffic with the Great Western at Swindon, and with the Swindon Marlborough & Andover's own southern section between Wolfhall Junction and Andover. There were, unfortunately, many delays before these goals could be achieved, and at the root of these problems was the Great Western Railway. In the early days, when it had seemed unlikely that the Swindon Marlborough & Andover would ever be built, the Great Western had been indifferent to its fate, but by the end of 1881 the old spectre of a north-to-south competitive route from Cheltenham and Andover was in danger of becoming a reality. Indeed, not only was the Swindon Marlborough & Andover line under construction, it had also successfully promoted an extension to the north, and was establishing close ties with the London & South Western Railway — an ambitious company that was, at that time, bent on aggression against the GWR.

The Swindon Marlborough & Andover company had no statutory running powers over the Great Western main line from Rushey Platt Junction to Swindon GW station, while the terms under which SM&A trains could use the lines between Marlborough and Wolfhall Junction had been left by the Swindon Marlborough & Andover Act of 1873 for future settlement, to be agreed with the owning companies (in effect the GWR) or failing that by arbitration. This left ample scope for hard bargaining and delay in the years ahead.

For facilities at Swindon the GWR demanded a payment of £5000, or £6000 for an easement over the junction at Rushey Platt, tolls calculated on a notional distance of six miles from the junction to Swindon station, instead of on the actual distance of 1 mile 18 chains, with a minimum payment of £900 per annum, plus £1500 per annum for the use of the station. These extortionate terms were whittled down on arbitration to £105 for the easement, two miles with a minimum of £200 in any one year for tolls, and £900 for the use of the station; but they were still a heavy burden for an impecunious concern such as the Swindon Marlborough & Andover Railway.

A passenger service between Swindon Town and Swindon (GW) was introduced on 6th February, 1882, but lasted only until 28th February, 1885 (inclusive), as it was running at a loss of nearly £1500 per annum. It was not restored until after grouping in 1923.

The obstacles between Marlborough and Wolfhall Junction were as much physical as financial. The steeply graded single line of the Marlborough Railway was worked on the wooden staff and ticket system, without any block telegraph instruments, while Savernake station, with only one through platform and very rudimentary signalling equipment, was described by a Board of Trade inspecting officer in March 1882 as 'not fit for the existing traffic, and still less for the additional traffic that would pass through it upon the opening of the new lines'.

This was in reference to the proposed opening throughout between Swindon and Andover, which the Swindon Marlborough & Andover company had perforce to defer until the GWR had put Savernake station in order and installed block telegraph on the Marlborough branch. This it was at length compelled to do, at the expense of the SM&A, under powers contained in the SM&A Act, 1882.

Meanwhile, the Swindon Marlborough & Andover put on a shuttle service between Grafton station, south of Wolfhall Junction, and Andover on 1st May, 1882, using a temporary connection with the L&SWR main line at Red Post Junction until 19th November, 1882, when the separate third road was brought into use. The newly opened section was single throughout with double-platform stations and crossing loops at Grafton, Collingbourne, Ludgershall, and Weyhill.

## Completion of the Swindon Marlborough & Andover

The improvements at Savernake station were finished in January 1883, and at the same time a lengthy dispute over terms for the use of the station and adjacent GWR lines was settled by an Arbitration Award (30th January, 1883), thereby enabling the SM&A to complete its initial undertaking and open throughout from Swindon to Andover on 5th February, 1883 — nearly ten years after the incorporation of the company.

The length of railway owned by the Swindon Marlborough & Andover company at the time of its completion totalled some 27½ route miles, namely, Rushey Platt Junction to Marlborough Junction 13 miles 47 chains; Wolfhall Junction to Red Post Junction 14 miles 1 chain, all of which was single track, except for the curve of 18 chains to the GWR at Rushey Platt Junction and about 30 chains from the north end of Marlborough Station to Marlborough Junction. The capital expenditure had mounted to over £600,000, and on top of that the company was committed to a costly and hazardous northern extension.

If the construction of the SM&A had followed the original plans from a junction at the east end of Swindon GWR station, it would have formed with the GW line to Gloucester and Cheltenham a through route, capable of attracting (so its optimistic promoters averred) some valuable through traffic, not only from the north but also from the coalfields of South Wales and the Forest of Dean. Indeed, it was claimed in early prospectuses of the SM&A that the line would make the construction of the Severn Tunnel unnecessary!

These sanguine hopes were not, of course, realised, and although the company did get some coal traffic for the L&SWR via Rushey Platt, the only hope of traffic in quantity sufficient to justify the capital cost lay in an independent extension to the north, with through facilities to the Midland Railway at Cheltenham — the completion, in effect, of Stephenson's original Manchester & Southampton scheme.

## The Swindon & Cheltenham Extension Railway

An extension line running northwards beyond the existing Swindon Marlborough & Andover railhead at Swindon had long been contemplated, and on 18th July, 1881 an Act was obtained to incorporate the 'Swindon & Cheltenham Extension Railway' as a nominally separate company, with power to build a main line from Rushey Platt to a junction at Andoversford with the Banbury & Cheltenham Direct Railway (the first section of which, worked by the GWR, had been opened on 1st June, 1881 as a single line from Lansdown Junction, Cheltenham, to Bourton-on-the-Water). A branch from Cirencester to Fairford, and a curve at Rushey Platt from the north towards Swindon Great Western station, were also authorised by the Swindon & Cheltenham Extension Act of 1881.

Troubles and misfortunes troubled the Swindon & Cheltenham from the very start. The Act of Incorporation was secured only after a costly battle in Parliament against the hostile Great Western, while a few months later the GWR took legal action to prevent the new company from gaining access to land required for bridges near Swindon. Moreover, the Swindon & Cheltenham Directors had embarked upon the construction of their line without any clear plan for the raising of capital, which was left very much to chance and to the devices of the contractors, Messrs Watson, Smith & Watson.

In the meantime, the struggling local companies placed great hopes upon the possibility of securing a full working agreement with the London & South Western Railway — which seemed to be following a policy of open warfare with the GWR. A joint deputation from the Swindon Marlborough & Andover and Swindon & Cheltenham companies conducted negotiations with the L&SWR in 1882, and powers which could have led to a working arrangement were included in the L&SWR draft Bill for 1883; but these were quickly dropped when the GWR and L&SWR decided to bury the hatchet and entered into an agreement (21st October, 1884) deliberately aimed to discourage the promotion of speculative and competitive railways in each other's territory.

The South Western defection did grave injury to the Swindon & Cheltenham Railway when it was already deeply in debt, with no part of the line open for traffic. A length of 13½ miles from the junction with the Swindon Marlborough & Andover at Rushey Platt to Cirencester was completed and opened on 18th December, 1883, but the immediate prospects of getting any further were extremely slight. The section opened was single track, though all bridges over and under the line were built for two tracks. There were intermediate stations at Rushey Platt, Cricklade, and Cerney, with crossing loops at the two first-named. A station for Blunsdon was opened on 1st September, 1895, and a crossing loop at Cerney in September 1900.

### Amalgamation

The Swindon & Cheltenham Extension Railway was worked by the Swindon Marlborough & Andover company under an agreement dated 10th June, 1882, and for all practical purposes it formed part of the SM&A from the outset. It was only a short step to a complete amalgamation of the two companies, effected under the Swindon, Marlborough & Andover and Swindon & Cheltenham Extension Railway Companies (Amalgamation) Act of 23rd June, 1884 (the operative date), section 4 of which enacted that 'the name of the amalgamated Company shall be The Midland & South Western Junction Railway Company'. This was the second railway company to bear this title; the first M&SWJR, incorporated in 1864, built the important loop line round the north-west outskirts of London from Cricklewood to Acton Wells Junction and was vested in the Midland Railway in 1874.

Meanwhile, a little work had been done on the extension north of Ciren-cester, where deviations from the original plans had been authorised by the S&CER Acts of 1883 and 1884. But the crisis was close at hand as funds ran out and creditors became more pressing. Messrs Watson, Smith & Watson, who went bankrupt in 1885, were released from their contract and departed from the scene in November 1884.

A Receiver was appointed on 20th December, 1884 on a petition of the company's own Engineer who had secured judgment against it for a debt of £5663 0s. 4d., and the newly formed Midland & South Western Junction Railway was left to face an apparently hopeless future of poverty and decay, unless by some means it could justify its title by linking up with the Midland Railway at Cheltenham.

In that direction also lay the only ray of hope for the company's creditors and stockholders, some of whom would have preferred to close the capital account, or even wind up the company altogether and obtain what they could from a sale of its assets. However, a majority eventually came out in favour of a bolder course. Some creditors agreed to accept, in satisfaction of their claims, 'B' Debenture Stock created and issued under the Midland & South Western Junction Act of 1886, and a further Act in 1887 allowed the company to issue £200,000 'A' Debenture Stock, ranking before every other class of stock, for the express purpose of completing the northern extension — a modest enough sum for 12 or 13 miles of line through the Cotswolds, including a tunnel at Chedworth and earthworks estimated at about 600,000 cubic yards of excavation.

## Completion to Cheltenham

Work was restarted north of Cirencester in May 1889, under a contract let to Charles Braddock, a Wigan-based contractor. Proceeding simultaneously from several different places, Mr Braddock made commendable progress on what was, after all, a comparatively difficult contract. The greatest obstacle between Cirencester and Andoversford was the 494 yds long Chedworth Tunnel, but there were in addition several large embankments and deep cuttings — including 60 ft embankments near Foss Cross and through Chedworth Woods.

Although horses, mechanical excavators and several Manning Wardle type saddle tank locomotives were used on the contract, much of the work relied on human muscle-power, and for this purpose the contractor em-ployed a small army of about 500 navvies. These gentlemen lived in a number of hutted camps beside the unfinished line, but generally speaking standards of accommodation and cleanliness were high, and local news-papers such as The Wilts & Glos Standard were impressed by the way in which Mr Braddock had provided for the comfort and well-being of his workforce. In 1889 a reporter from the Standard visited the works, and noted that the navvies' huts were each presided over by a 'landlord' and 'landlady':

> These wooden houses are comfortable structures and consist of a private room for the landlord, landlady and family; a good-sized, commodious, well-lighted, well-heated general dayroom for the men; a bedroom of about similar dimensions containing eight or ten comfortable beds which the lodgers occupy in pairs. The men purchase their own meat from the butcher as he calls, the landlady cooking it for them and supplying them with bread, grocery and other necessaries. On the occasion of the recent visit some of the men were amusing themselves with reading, cards, dominoes and so forth while others had retired early to rest in preparation for the morrow's labours. They begin work at 6 o'clock and the landlady prepares breakfast for them before they turn out. In the pointed roof were hung the men's changes of linen in readiness for the coming Sunday, and the garments were evidently well-tended and could not fail to be well-aired, while the tobacco smoke doubtless scared away the moth!

Sadly, the works did not proceed without accident, one of the most serious, (and indeed spectacular) incidents being a bridge failure that occurred in Chedworth Woods when a construction train was passing along the temporary contractor's way; the locomotive left the rails and fell thirty feet into the woods below, killing its unfortunate driver. This incident was, needless to say, a matter of considerable controversy, and much blame was subsequently attached to the Earl of Eldon who (doubtless for the best possible reasons) had delayed completion of the failed bridge in an attempt to divert the railway away from the nearby Chedworth Roman Villa.

The Cheltenham extension was more or less complete by the summer of 1890, but when the railway was nearly ready for opening in June 1890 a portion of Chedworth Tunnel fell in, bringing down about 60 ft depth of earth, and leading to an inevitable dispute over responsibility. The tunnel collapse was soon put right, but further problems ensued when an underline bridge to the north of Chedworth failed in February 1891. Moreover, the completion of the junction at Andoversford was held up by the inevitable delay in agreeing terms with the Great Western for the use of the line to Lansdown Junction, Cheltenham, over which the Midland & South Western Junction Railway had running powers under the Swindon & Cheltenham Extension Act of 1881 (confirmed by the M&SWJ Act, 1889).

A further problem arose because accommodation was not yet available for Midland & South Western Junction traffic at the Midland station in Cheltenham. Goods traffic nevertheless started in a small way as far as Dowdeswell on 16th March, 1891, mainly as a sop to impatient creditors; the full opening was delayed until 1st August, 1891, when M&SWJ passenger trains started to run through to Cheltenham (Midland). A few weeks previously, on 30th June, 1891, what was apparently the very first through passenger train had traversed the line when over four hundred excursionists were taken on an outing from Marlborough to Birmingham.

The final link of 13¾ miles north of Cirencester was single track, except between Dowdeswell station and Andoversford Junction, but it was equipped for operation with Tyer's electric tablet apparatus, instead of the wooden staff and ticket system in use elsewhere on the M&SWJ at that time.

In addition to Dowdeswell, there were stations and crossing loops at Foss Cross and Withington; a single-platform station was opened at Chedworth on 1st October, 1892. Chedworth tunnel (494 yds) and all the overbridges were built to double-line width, but the engineering works as a whole were kept to a bare minimum to save cost.

Accommodation for M&SWJ traffic at Cheltenham was secured by enlarging the Midland station at Lansdown for passenger trains, and by acquiring land in Alstone for sidings and a goods yard adjacent to High Street (Midland) goods station. These works were carried out under the Cheltenham Station Act (14th August, 1890), which was promoted by two Directors of the M&SWJ to incorporate a separate body called the Cheltenham Station Company with a capital of £20,000. Most of this sum appears to have been found by the Midland Railway, which undertook the necessary works and subsequently absorbed the Cheltenham Station Company in 1895, when a comprehensive agreement with the M&SWJ governing the maintenance and extent of its facilities at Cheltenham was concluded.

At the southern end of the M&SWJ full running powers over the L&SWR from Andover Junction to Southampton Docks had been obtained under the SM&A Act, 1882 (section 34) — a most valuable right enjoyed by no other company. They were exercised for goods traffic from 1st November, 1892 and for regular passenger trains, worked by M&SWJ engines and crews, from 1st June, 1894.

As an example of railway engineering, the completed Midland & South Western Junction line lacked those marks of distinction which were so conspicuous in the continuously heavy earthworks, good alignment, and moderately even gradients of its near neighbour (and former rival), the Didcot, Newbury & Southampton Railway.

Both lines were built through difficult country from very meagre resources, but the DN&S had the services of a famous Engineer, Sir John Fowler (1817–98), throughout from Didcot to Winchester, whereas the M&SWJ was put together in bits and pieces under the guidance of several engineers. G. P. Bidder was Consulting Engineer to the SM&A, but he died in 1878, before construction had started in earnest. He was succeeded by W. J. Kingsbury on the SM&A and Charles Liddell on the Cheltenham Extension. Any unifying influence was supplied by J. R. Shopland, who came as Resident Engineer to the Swindon Marlborough & Andover in 1875 and remained with the M&SWJ until his death in 1897. After an interval, during which R. St. G. Moore had supervised the construction of the Marlborough & Grafton Railway, E. Connal came to the company in charge of the widening works, commenced in 1899, and was officially appointed Engineer in 1903, holding office until 1923.

The heaviest earthworks were between Marlborough tunnel* and Rushey Platt, and again between Foss Cross and Andoversford. Elsewhere they were fairly light, sometimes at the expense of the alignment. Reverse curvature was most prevalent in the Cotswolds north of Cirencester, where it could hardly have been avoided with the scanty funds available for construction, but at some other points it was less excusable; a number of deviations south of Marlborough were put in to suit the requirements of landowners.

---

* See Chapter Two for details of the Marlborough & Grafton line.

Midland & South Western Junction Railway architecture was plain and unpretentious; the company's stations had a certain family likeness, but no special features other than the rather prominent chimney stacks most noticeable at Swindon and Marlborough. The station building at Cirencester was faced with stone, but the material most commonly favoured for structures in general was red brick, not perhaps of a very enduring quality, as it was necessary to carry out extensive relining works in Marlborough tunnel in 1925, and again in 1944.

There were, broadly speaking, just two basic types of station building on the M&SWJ system — a 'large' design, found only at Swindon, Cricklade and Marlborough, and a smaller, simpler design found elsewhere. Most of the stations had hipped roofs and projecting canopies, but Foss Cross and Withington had gable-ended roofs and no canopies. External woodwork was probably painted dark buff, but some platform canopies sported a 'striped' colour scheme incorporating alternate light and dark-coloured vertical planking (the colours used may have been light and dark buff).

The largest bridge on the Midland & South Junction line — the one across the Great Western at Rushey Platt — was constructed with a span of 92½ ft composed of wrought iron girders resting on masonry abutments. Four of the overbridges between Rushey Platt and Cirencester had arched approaches instead of the usual earth ramps, three of them with ten spans and one with nine spans.

MIDLAND AND SOUTH WESTERN
JUNCTION RAILWAY.

CHELTENHAM
·THE·GARDEN·TOWN·

Colleges.                    Health &
Golf.                        Pleasure
Hunting.                     Resort.
OPEN·AIR·CONCERTS·DAILY.
UNSURPASSED·RESIDENTIAL·CENTRE
MINERAL·WATERS & MEDICAL·BATHS.

For particulars of the Train Service to Cheltenham see
the Company's Time Tables and Notices.
Photochrom

A view looking towards the north end of Chedworth Tunnel during the early stages of construction.                                    *Norman Irvine Collection*

Swindon Town station from the north, as seen on an early postcard of 1905, when enlargement of the station was nearly complete.                    *Author's Collection*

*M. and S.W.R. Station, Old Swindon*

# TIME TABLE OF LOCAL TRAINS.

## CHELTENHAM, SWINDON, MARLBOROUGH, ANDOVER JUNCTION & SOUTHAMPTON.

For Service of Trains with the Midland system see pages 4, 5, 6 & 7; L. & S.W. system, pages 4, 5, 6 & 7; L. & S.W. system, pages 4, 5, 8 & 9; L. & N.W. system, pages 10 & 11; and G.W. system, pages 12 & 13.
ALL M. & S.W.J. TRAINS ARE FIRST AND THIRD CLASS ONLY.

### STATIONS — WEEK DAYS

| Stations | a.m. | a.m. | a.m. | a.m. | a.m. | a.m. | a.m. | a.m. | a.m. | a.m. | p.m. | p.m. | p.m. | p.m. | p.m. | p.m. | p.m. | p.m. |
|---|---|---|---|---|---|---|---|---|---|---|---|---|---|---|---|---|---|---|
| Cheltenham ... dep. | 4 50 | | | | | 6 15 | | | 9 36 | 10 37 | | | | | | | | |
| Chltnm & Lk'mpt'n | | | | | | | | | 9 40 | | | | | | | | | |
| Charlton Kings | | | | | | | | | 9 45 | | | | | | | | | |
| Andoversford Junc. | | | | | | | | | 9 58 | | | | | | | | | |
| Andrvsfd & Dwdswll | | | | | | 5 46 | | | 10 6 | | | | | | | | | |
| Withington | | | | | | | | | 10 15 | | | | | | | | | |
| Chedworth | | | | | | | | | 10 19 | 11 20 | | | | | | | | |
| Foss Cross | | | | | | 6 7 | | | 10 35 | | | | | | | | | |
| Cirencester | | | | | | 6 16 | | | 10 42 | | | | | | | | | |
| Cerney | | | | | | 6 25 | | | 10 50 | | | | | | | | | |
| Crickdale | | | | | | 6 35 | | | 10 55 | | | | | | | | | |
| Blunsdon | | | | | | 6 47 | | | 11 5 | 11 47 | | | | | | | | |
| Swindon Town ... arr. | 6 0 | | | | | | | | | | | | | | | | | |
| Swindon Town ... dep. | 6 25 | | | | 6 55 | | 9 30 | 9 45 | 11 50 | | 12 16 | | | | | | | |
| Chiseldon | | | | | | 6 1 | 9 14 | 9 52 | | | 12 23 | | | | | | | |
| Ogbourne | | | | | | 6 15 | 9 23 | 10 0 | | | 12 29 | | | | | | | |
| Marlborough | | 7 38 | | | | 6 32 | 9 35 | 3 10 | 12 10 | 12 36 | | | | | | | | |
| Savernake | | | | | | 6 52 | 9 51 | | 12 20 | 12 46 | | | | | | | | |
| Gratton & Burbage. | | | | | | 7 0 | 10 0 | | | | | | | | | | | |
| Collingbourne | | | | | | 8 0 | 10 5 | | 12 31 | | | | | | | | | |
| Ludgershall ... arr. | 7 25 | | | | 8 27 | | | | | 12 52 | | | | | | | | |
| Tidworth { arr. | 7 25 | 7 38 | | | 8 27 | | | | | | | | | | | | | |
| Tidworth { dep. | 7 30 | 7 38 | | | | | | | | | | | | | | | | |
| Ludgershall ... dep. | | 7 45 | 8 0 | 9 52 | | | | | 12 36 | | | | | | | | | |
| Weyhill | | 7 53 | | 10 1 | | | | | 12 40 | | | | | | | | | |
| Andover Junction ... arr. | | 7 59 | 8 20 | 10 3 10 | | | | | 12 46 | | | | | | | | | |
| Andover Junction ... dep. | 7 30 | | 8 25 | 9 12 | | | | | 12 56 | | | | | | | | | |
| Andover Town | | | | 9 16 | | | | | 1 0 | | | | | | | | | |
| Clatford | | | | 9 21 | | | | | 1 5 | | | | | | | | | |
| Fullerton | | | | 9 28 | | | | | | | | | | | | | | |
| Stockbridge | | | | 9 36 | | | | | 1 21 | | | | | | | | | |
| Horsebridge | | | | 9 43 | | | | | 1 29 | | | | | | | | | |
| Mottisfont | | | | 9 49 | | | | | 1 36 | | | | | | | | | |
| Romsey | | | | 9 56 | | | | | 1 42 | | | | | | | | | |
| Nursling | | | | | | | | | 1 49 | | | | | | | | | |
| Redbridge | | | | | | | | | 2 11 | | | | | | | | | |
| Millbrook | | | | | | | | | 2 14 | | | | | | | | | |
| Southampton West arr. | 8 12 | | | | | 9 8 | | | 1 39 | | | | | | | | | |
| Southampton Docks | 8 21 | | | | | 9 16 | 10 27 | 12 45 | 1 48 | | | | | | | | | |

(Through services noted in table: "Through Express Nottingham and Birmingham to Southampton"; "Through Express Manchester L. & N.W. to Southampton, &c."; "South Express"; "See Page 4."; "See Page 11.")

### SUNDAYS

| Stations | p.m. | p.m. | p.m. | p.m. |
|---|---|---|---|---|
| Cheltenham ... dep. | 3 15 | 5 15 | | 7 15 |
| Charlton Kings | 3 34 | | | |
| Andoversford Junc. | 3 39 | | | |
| Andrvsfd & Dwdswll | 3 47 | 5 50 | | |
| Withington | 3 51 | | | |
| Foss Cross | 4 5 | 6 0 50 | 2 45 | |
| Cirencester | 4 14 | 6 58 | 2 52 | |
| Cerney | 4 23 | 7 10 | | |
| Crickdale | 4 29 | 7 20 | | |
| Blunsdon | 4 41 | 7 42 | 3 10 | |
| Swindon Town ... arr. | | | | |
| Swindon Town ... dep. | 4 50 | 7 50 | | 7 40 |
| Chiseldon | 4 57 | 6 58 8 0 | | |
| Ogbourne | | 8 11 3 0 | | 5 52 |
| Marlborough | 5 14 | 8 22 3 10 | | 6 4 |
| Savernake | 5 24 | 8 31 | | |
| Gratton & Burbage. | 5 34 | 8 44 | | |
| Collingbourne | 5 45 | 8 54 | | |
| Ludgershall ... arr. | 5 50 | 8 59 | | |
| Tidworth { arr. | | 9 12 | | |
| Tidworth { dep. | | 8 45 | | |
| Ludgershall ... dep. | 5 52 | 9 1 | | 7 7 |
| Weyhill | | 9 11 | | 7 14 |
| Andover Junction ... arr. | 6 4 | 9 20 | | 7 20 |
| Andover Junction ... dep. | 6 32 | 9 50 | | |
| Andover Town | 6 36 | 9 54 | | |
| Clatford | 6 41 | 9 59 | | |
| Fullerton | 6 49 | 10 6 | | |
| Stockbridge | 6 57 | 10 14 | | |
| Horsebridge | 7 5 | 10 22 | | |
| Mottisfont | 7 12 | 10 29 | | |
| Romsey | 7 22 | 10 38 | | |
| Nursling | 7 29 | 10 45 | | |
| Redbridge | 7 31 | 10 50 | | |
| Millbrook | 7 39 | 10 55 | | |
| Southampton West arr. | 7 42 | 10 58 | | |
| Southampton Docks | 7 52 | 11 6 | | |

A—Stops at Cricklade on Saturdays and on Cricklade Market Days.   B—Arrives Cirencester 6.7 a.m.   D—Arrives Cirencester 10.50 a.m.
s—Saturdays only; on other week-days arrive Southampton Docks at 10.42 p.m. via Basingstoke.   s—Saturdays only.

**For Local Service between Swindon and Chiseldon see page 13.**

Local MSWJ Passenger Service for 12th July, 1915 from their own timetable.

# TIME TABLE OF LOCAL TRAINS.

## SOUTHAMPTON, ANDOVER JUNCTION, MARLBOROUGH, SWINDON & CHELTENHAM.

For Service of Trains with the Midland system see pages 4, 5, 6 & 7; L. & S.W. system, pages 4, 5, 6 & 7; L. & S.W. system, pages 4, 5, 8 & 9; L. & N.W. system, pages 10 & 11; and G.W. system, pages 12 & 13.
ALL M. & S.W.J. TRAINS ARE FIRST AND THIRD CLASS ONLY.

| STATIONS. | WEEK DAYS. | | | | | | | | | | | | | | | | | SUNDAYS. | | | | | | | | |
|---|---|---|---|---|---|---|---|---|---|---|---|---|---|---|---|---|---|---|---|---|---|---|---|---|---|

*Week-day and Sunday times as printed. Column headings include "North Express" and through-express notes:*

- Through Express Southampton to Manchester, L. & N.W. Railway, &c.
- Through Express Southampton to Birmingham and Derby.
- See Pages 5 & 10.

**Stations (reading down):**

- Southampton Docks .......... dep.
- Southampton West "
- Millbrook "
- Redbridge "
- Nursling "
- Romsey "
- Mottisfont "
- Horsebridge "
- Stockbridge "
- Fullerton "
- Chatford "
- Andover Town "
- Andover Junction .......... arr.
- Andover Junction .......... dep.
- Weyhill "
- Ludgershall .......... arr.
- Tidworth { arr. / dep. }
- Ludgershall .......... dep.
- Collingbourne "
- Grafton & Burbage "
- Savernake "
- Marlborough "
- Ogbourne "
- Chiseldon "
- Swindon Town .......... arr.
- Swindon Town .......... dep.
- Blunsdon "
- Cricklade "
- Cerney "
- Cirencester "
- Foss Cross "
- Chedworth "
- Withington "
- Andoxfeld & Dowdeswell "
- Andverford Junction "
- Charlton Kings "
- Cheltenham S. & L'k'n pl'n "
- Cheltenham .......... arr.

A.—Stops at Ludgershall to pick up Passengers only.

H.C.—Horse Boxes, Carriage Trucks, &c., are not conveyed by these Trains except from L. S. W. Line to Cheltenham and Stations beyond.

**For Local Service between Swindon and Chiseldon see page 13.**

## CHELTENHAM, CIRENCESTER, SWINDON, MARLBOROUGH, and ANDOVER.

*Offices*—Swindon. Midland and South Western Junction. Gen. Man., J. Davies.

| Miles | Down. | Week Days. Saturdays only. Ocean Boat Express. | Sunday night and Monday morning. / Except Sunday night and Monday morning. | | | | Saturdays only. | | Mondays only. | | Except Saturdays. | | | Weds. and Sats. / Sats. only. Marlboro' | | | | Sundays. | | | | |
|---|---|---|---|---|---|---|---|---|---|---|---|---|---|---|---|---|---|---|---|---|---|---|
| — | **Cheltenham** § ......dep. | 4 50 | 5 0 | .... | .... | 1032 | | 1 15 | | 3 5 | | 4 55 | 6 55 | | .... | .... | .... | 6 0 | .... | .... | .... | .... |
| 2 | Cheltenham South ** .. | | .... | .... | .... | 1038 | | 1 21 | | .... | | 5 1 | 7 1 | | .... | .... | .... | .... | .... | .... | .... | .... |
| 3¼ | Charlton Kings ........ | | .... | .... | .... | .... | | 1 25 | | d | | .... | 7 6 | | .... | .... | .... | .... | .... | .... | .... | .... |
| 7 | Andoversford Junc. .... | | .... | .... | .... | .... | | .... | | .... | | .... | .... | | .... | .... | .... | .... | .... | .... | .... | .... |
| 7¾ | Andoversford & Dowdeswell | | .... | .... | .... | 1051 | | 1 36 | | 3 22 | | 5 16 | 7 19 | | .... | .... | .... | 6 20 | .... | .... | .... | .... |
| 9¾ | Withington .......[well | | .... | .... | .... | .... | | 1 41 | | .... | | 5 20 | 7 25 | | .... | .... | .... | 6 26 | .... | .... | .... | .... |
| 13¾ | Chedworth ............ | | 5 30 | .... | .... | 11 1 | | 1 49 | | 3 35 | | 5 30 | 7 33 | | .... | .... | .... | 6 34 | .... | .... | .... | .... |
| 14¾ | Foss Cross ............ | | .... | .... | .... | .... | | .... | | | | .... | 7 37 | | .... | .... | .... | 6 38 | .... | .... | .... | .... |
| 20¾ | **Cirencester** ‖ **83** ...... | | 5 50 | .... | 8 15 | 1114 | | 2 2 | | 3 49 | | 5 45 | 7 52 | | .... | .... | .... | 6 55 | .... | 3 56 | .... | .... |
| 23¾ | Cerney & Ashton Keynes | | 6 0 | .... | 8 24 | .... | | 2 9 | | .... | | 5 53 | 8 0 | | .... | .... | .... | 7 3 | .... | 4 4 | .... | .... |
| 27¼ | Cricklade ............ | | 6 13 | .... | 8 36 | 1127 | | 2 17 | | .... | | 6 3 | 8 13 | | .... | .... | .... | 7 15 | .... | 4 17 | .... | .... |
| 29¾ | Blunsdon ............ | | 6 21 | .... | 8 44 | .... | | .... | | .... | | .... | 8 20 | | .... | .... | .... | 7 23 | .... | 4 25 | .... | .... |
| 35¾ | **Swindon Town** .. arr. | 6 5 | 6 32 | .... | 8 55 | 1141 | .... | 2 32 | .... | 4 12 | .... | 6 18 | 8 31 | | .... | .... | .... | 7 47 | .... | 4 43 | .... | .... |
| | dep. | 6 10 | 6 40 | 8 0 | 9 10 | 1144 | 1 15 | 2 35 | 3 30 | 4 15 | 6 0 | 6 25 | 8 38 | 1110 | .... | .... | .... | 7 52 | 2 45 | 4 50 | 8 0 | .... |
| 38¾ | Chiseldon ............ | | 6 50 | 8 6 | 9 19 | .... | 1 22 | 2 42 | 3 38 | .... | 6 7 | 6 33 | 8 48 | 1117 | .... | .... | .... | 8 2 | 2 52 | 4 59 | 8 8 | .... |
| 42¼ | Ogbourne ............ | | 6 59 | .... | 9 28 | .... | .... | 2 50 | 3 45 | .... | .... | 6 42 | 8 58 | .... | .... | .... | .... | 8 11 | 3 0 | 5 9 | .... | .... |
| 47 | **Marlborough** ........ | | 7 10 | .... | 9 42 | 12 4 | .... | 3 0 | 3 56 | 4 36 | .... | 6 53 | 9 10 | 1137 | .... | .... | .... | 8 22 | 3 12 | 5 20 | 8 24 | .... |
| 52¼ | **Savernake 30, 33** .... | | 7 23 | .... | 9 52 | 1214 | .... | 3 10 | .... | 4 46 | .... | 7 4 | 9 22 | 1148 | .... | .... | .... | 8 37 | 3 23 | 5 33 | 8 35 | .... |
| 54¼ | Grafton and Burbage... | | 7 32 | .... | 9 58 | .... | .... | 3 15 | .... | .... | .... | 7 12 | .... | .... | .... | .... | .... | 8 44 | .... | 5 41 | .... | .... |
| 58½ | Collingbourne ........ | | 7 42 | .... | 10 7 | Fri. | .... | 3 24 | .... | .... | .... | 7 22 | .... | .... | .... | .... | .... | 8 54 | .... | 5 51 | .... | .... |
| 61 | Ludgershall ........ | | 7 49 | .... | 1013 | 1228 | .... | 3 32 | .... | 5 2 | .... | 7 29 | 9 38 | 12 3 | .... | .... | .... | 9 1 | 3 39 | 5 58 | 8 49 | .... |
| 63½ | **Tidworth** ........arr. | | 8 43 | .... | 1021 | 1235 | .... | 4 28 | .... | 5 26 | .... | 8 21 | 1043 | 1215 | .... | .... | .... | 9 11 | 3 50 | 6 49 | 9 0 | .... |
| 65 | Weyhill ..[105, 125, 126 | | .... | .... | 1021 | .... | .... | 3 41 | .... | .... | .... | 7 37 | .... | .... | .... | .... | .... | 9 11 | .... | .... | .... | .... |
| 68½ | **Andover** Junc. **102**, arr. | 7 12 | 8 1 | .... | 1028 | 1238 | .... | 3 48 | .... | 5 14 | .... | 7 43 | 9 50 | .... | .... | .... | .... | 9.20 | .... | 6 10 | .... | .... |
| 96½ | **126** Southampton ¶ arr. | 8 12 | 9l16 | .... | 1238 | 1 27 | .... | 5 20 | .... | 6 13 | .... | .... | .... | .... | .... | .... | .... | 11 4 | .... | 7 54 | .... | .... |
| 123½ | **128** Portsmouth (Tn) " | 9 25 | 1140 | .... | .... | 3k20 | .... | 6 36 | .... | 8 16 | .... | | | .... | .... | .... | .... | 12k44 | .... | 9 21 | .... | .... |
| 118½ | **108** Bournem'th (C.) " | 9 24 | 1049 | .... | 3 9 | 3 9 | .... | 7 4 | .... | 7 32 | .... | .... | .... | .... | .... | .... | .... | 2 42 | .... | 10 3 | .... | .... |
| 85½ | **102** Salisbury ..... " | 8 7 | 9 37 | .... | 11 2 | 1 12 | .... | 4 33 | .... | 6 53 | .... | 8 22 | 1054 | .... | .... | .... | .... | 1133 | .... | 8 53 | .... | .... |
| 135 | **105 London** (Wat.).. " | .... | 1011 | .... | 1 37 | 2 32 | .... | 6 15 | .... | 7 31 | .... | 1034 | .... | .... | .... | .... | .... | 12 5 | .... | 8 0 | .... | .... |

*b* Friday night times.
*c* Through Carriages to Southampton.
**d** Stops by Signal to take up.
*g* Leaves at 12 25 mrn. on Mondays.
*h* Except Mondays.
*i* Leaves Belfast at 9 aft. except Sunday nights.
*k* Via Southampton.
*l* Arrives at 10 33 mrn. on Saturdays.
* Market Street.
† Station Road.
‡ New Street.
§ Queen's Road, Lansdown.
‖ Watermoor; over ½ mile to Sheep Street Station (G.W.).
¶ Town and Dock Station; calls at **West Station** about 5 mins. *earlier*.
** Cheltenham South and Leckhampton.

## TIDWORTH and ANDOVER JUNCTION.—Midland and South Western Junction.

| Miles | Down. | Week Days. mrn | mrn | mrn | mrn | Sats. aft | aft | aft | aft | aft | Sats. aft | | | | | Sundays. mrn | mrn | aft | aft | aft | aft |
|---|---|---|---|---|---|---|---|---|---|---|---|---|---|---|---|---|---|---|---|---|---|
| | **Tidworth** ..........dep. | 7 30 | 8 50 | 10 0 | 1145 | 1 33 | 2 32 | 3 10 | 4 50 | 7 15 | 1050 | .... | .... | .... | .... | 8 45 | 1140 | 1 30 | 5 40 | 7 0 | 9 10 |
| 2½ | Ludgershall ...... arr. | 7 36 | 8 56 | 10 6 | 1151 | 1 41 | 2 38 | 3 16 | 4 56 | 7 21 | 1056 | .... | .... | .... | .... | 8 52 | 1147 | 1 36 | 5 46 | 7 6 | 9 16 |
| | dep. | 7 37 | .... | 1013 | 1228 | 1 42 | .... | 3 17 | 5 2 | 7 29 | 1057 | .... | .... | .... | .... | 9 1 | .... | .... | 5 58 | 7 7 | .... |
| 6¼ | Weyhill ..........[105 | 7 45 | .... | 1021 | .... | 1 50 | .... | 3 25 | .... | 7 37 | .... | .... | .... | .... | .... | 9 11 | .... | .... | .... | 7 15 | .... |
| 9¾ | **Andover** Junc. **102**, arr. | 7 51 | .... | 1028 | 1238 | 1 56 | .... | 3 32 | 5 14 | 7 43 | 11 9 | .... | .... | .... | .... | 9 20 | .... | .... | 6 10 | 7 21 | .... |

## ANDOVER, MARLBOROUGH, SWINDON, CIRENCESTER, and CHELTENHAM.

Sec., E. T. Lawrence.] Midland and South Western Junction. [Traff. Supt., J. M. Malerbi.

| Miles | Station | | | | | North Express. | | Saturdays only. | North Express. | Saturdays only. | Mondays only. | | Except Saturdays. | | Thursdays only. | | | | | Sundays | | | |
|---|---|---|---|---|---|---|---|---|---|---|---|---|---|---|---|---|---|---|---|---|---|---|---|
| — | **Andover** Junc. ....dep. | .... | 5 50 | .... | 8 50 | 1144 | 1155 | | 2 34 | .... | .... | 5 0 | .... | 7 55 | | .... | .... | .... | .... | 1130 | .... | 6 30 | 8 25 |
| 3½ | Weyhill ............ | .... | .... | .... | .... | .... | 12 3 | | .... | .... | .... | 5 8 | .... | 8 3 | | .... | .... | .... | .... | 1139 | .... | .... | 8 35 |
| — | **Tidworth** ........dep. | .... | .... | .... | 8 50 | 1145 | 1145 | | 2 32 | 3 10 | .... | 4 50 | | 7 15 | | .... | .... | .... | .... | 1140 | 1 30 | 5 40 | 7 0 |
| 7¼ | Ludgershall ............ | .... | 6 10 | .... | 9 5 | 1157 | 1212 | | 2 45 | 3 45 | .... | 5 17 | | 8 11 | | .... | .... | .... | .... | 1150 | 1 41 | 6 48 | 8 46 |
| 9¾ | Collingbourne ........ | .... | .... | .... | 9 11 | .... | 1219 | | .... | 3 51 | .... | 5 23 | | 8 17 | | .... | .... | .... | .... | 1159 | .... | .... | 8 54 |
| 14 | Grafton and Burbage... | .... | .... | .... | 9 20 | .... | 1229 | | .... | 4 0 | .... | 5 32 | | 8 26 | | .... | .... | .... | .... | 1211 | .... | .... | 9 5 |
| 16 | **Savernake 30, 33** .... | .... | 6 31 | .... | 9 26 | .... | 1235 | | .... | 4 5 | .... | 5 37 | | 8 33 | | .... | .... | .... | .... | 1220 | .... | 7 4 | 9 11 |
| 21½ | **Marlborough** ........ | .... | 6 48 | .... | 9 39 | 1220 | 1245 | | 3 6 | 4 15 | 4 15 | 5 48 | | 8 45 | | .... | .... | .... | .... | 1234 | 2 5 | 7 16 | 9 25 |
| 26 | Ogbourne ............ | .... | 7 0 | .... | 9 49 | .... | 1256 | | .... | 4 26 | 4 26 | 5 59 | | 8 58 | | .... | .... | .... | .... | 1248 | .... | .... | 9 37 |
| 29½ | Chiseldon ............ | 5 20 | 7 9 | 8 15 | 9 58 | .... | 1 6 | 1 40 | .... | 4 36 | 4 36 | 6 8 | 6 45 | 9 8 | | .... | .... | .... | .... | 1 0 | 2 20 | 7 33 | 9 48 |
| 32¾ | **Swindon Town** .. arr. | 5 27 | 7 16 | 8 21 | 10 4 | 1240 | 1 12 | 1 47 | 3 25 | 4 42 | 4 42 | 6 15 | 6 52 | 9 15 | | .... | .... | .... | .... | 1 8 | 2 27 | 7 40 | 9 55 |
| | dep. | .... | 7 26 | .... | 10 8 | 1243 | 1 18 | .... | 3 27 | | | 6 20 | .... | 9 25 | 1110 | .... | .... | .... | .... | 1 30 | .... | .... | 10 0 |
| 38½ | Blunsdon ............ | .... | .... | .... | .... | .... | 1 29 | .... | .... | | | 6 31 | .... | .... | .... | .... | .... | .... | .... | 1 49 | .... | .... | .... |
| 41 | Cricklade ............ | .... | 7 45 | .... | 1023 | .... | 1 35 | .... | .... | | | 6 37 | .... | 9 42 | 1126 | .... | .... | .... | .... | 2 0 | .... | .... | 1016 |
| 44½ | Cerney & Ashton Keynes | .... | 7 54 | .... | 1031 | .... | 1 43 | .... | .... | | | 6 46 | .... | 9 50 | 1134 | .... | .... | .... | .... | 2 8 | .... | .... | 1025 |
| 47½ | **Cirencester** ‖ **83** ...... | .... | 8 3 | .... | 1038 | 1 7 | 1 52 | .... | 3 49 | | | 6 55 | .... | 9 57 | 1140 | .... | .... | .... | .... | 2 15 | .... | .... | 1033 |
| 53¾ | Foss Cross ............ | .... | 8 16 | .... | .... | | 2 5 | .... | | | | 7 9 | .... | .... | .... | .... | .... | .... | .... | .... | .... | .... | .... |
| 55 | Chedworth ............ | .... | 8 20 | .... | 1054 | | 2 9 | .... | | | | 7 14 | .... | .... | .... | .... | .... | .... | .... | .... | .... | .... | 1049 |
| 58½ | Withington .......[well | .... | 8 27 | .... | 11 1 | | 2 17 | .... | | | | 7 23 | .... | .... | .... | .... | .... | .... | .... | .... | .... | .... | 1058 |
| 60¾ | Andoversford & Dowdeswell | .... | 8 32 | .... | 11 6 | | 2 22 | .... | | | | 7 29 | .... | .... | .... | .... | .... | .... | .... | .... | .... | .... | .... |
| 61½ | Andoversford Junc. .... | .... | .... | .... | .... | | 2 24 | .... | | .... | .... | .... | .... | .... | .... | .... | .... | .... | .... | .... | .... | .... | .... |
| 65 | Charlton Kings ........ | .... | 8 43 | .... | .... | | 2 33 | .... | | .... | .... | 7 39 | .... | .... | .... | .... | .... | .... | .... | .... | .... | .... | .... |
| 66¾ | Cheltenham Sth.** [552 | .... | 8 47 | .... | .... | | 2 38 | .... | | .... | .... | 7 44 | .... | .... | .... | .... | .... | .... | .... | .... | .... | .... | .... |
| 68½ | **Cheltenham § 57**, arr. | .... | 8 52 | .... | 1120 | 1 42 | 2 43 | .... | 4 20 | .... | .... | 7 50 | .... | .... | .... | .... | .... | .... | .... | .... | .... | .... | 1118 |
| 90 | **552** Worcest'r (S.H.) arr. | .... | 10 2 | .... | 1235 | .... | 3 35 | .... | 5 27 | .... | .... | 9 6 | .... | .... | .... | .... | .... | .... | .... | .... | .... | .... | .... |
| 113¾ | **552** Birmingham ‡.. " | .... | 11 5 | .... | 1248 | 3 0 | 4 22 | .... | 5 40 | .... | .... | 9 55 | .... | .... | .... | .... | .... | .... | .... | .... | .... | .... | .... |
| 156 | **553** Derby ........ " | .... | 1232 | .... | 1 42 | 4 3 | 5 26 | .... | 6 50 | .... | .... | 1132 | .... | .... | .... | .... | .... | .... | .... | .... | .... | .... | .... |
| 217½ | **553** Manchester (C) " | .... | 2 35 | .... | 5 15 | 6 20 | 7 15 | .... | 8 40 | .... | .... | 2h35 | .... | .... | .... | .... | .... | .... | .... | .... | .... | .... | .... |
| 192¼ | **553** Sheffield † ... " | .... | 1 42 | .... | 3 30 | 5 13 | 6 25 | .... | 7 53 | .... | .... | 1230 | .... | .... | .... | .... | .... | .... | .... | .... | .... | .... | .... |
| 238¾ | **553** York ........ " | .... | 3 0 | .... | 5 50 | 6 0 | 7 45 | .... | 10 0 | .... | .... | 3 31 | .... | .... | .... | .... | .... | .... | .... | .... | .... | .... | .... |
| 231½ | **553** Leeds (Well.) .. " | .... | 3 0 | .... | 3 12 | 6 40 | 7 25 | .... | 8 57 | .... | .... | 1 25 | .... | .... | .... | .... | .... | .... | .... | .... | .... | .... | .... |
| 245½ | **553** Bradford * .... " | .... | .... | .... | 3 45 | 7 28 | 7 53 | .... | 9 50 | .... | .... | 2 50 | .... | .... | .... | .... | .... | .... | .... | .... | .... | .... | .... |
| 303½ | **553** Heysham ...... " | .... | .... | .... | 6 38 | .... | 1015 | .... | 11½c | .... | .... | .... | .... | .... | .... | .... | .... | .... | .... | .... | .... | .... | .... |
| 344½ | **553** Carlisle (Citdl) " | .... | .... | .... | 5 50 | .... | .... | .... | 1725 | .... | .... | 4 15 | .... | .... | .... | .... | .... | .... | .... | .... | .... | .... | .... |

*a* Through Carriages, Southampton to Birmingham and Derby.
*b* Bournemouth (West), via Salisbury.
*c* Arrives Belfast at 6 mrn.
**d** Through Carriages from Southampton to Birmingham, Derby, and Sheffield.
*g* Via Southampton.
*h* Arrives at 3 10 mrn. on Sundays.
*i* Except Sundays.
* Market Street. † Station Road.
‡ New Street.
§ Queen's Road, Lansdown; 1¼ miles to St. James's Square Station (G. W.).
‖ Watermoor Station: over ½ mile to Sheep Street Station (G. W.).
¶ Town and Dock Station; calls at **West Station** about 5 minutes later.
** Cheltenham South and Leckhampton.

## ANDOVER JUNCTION and TIDWORTH.—Midland and South Western Junction.

| Miles | Up. | Week Days. mrn | mrn | mrn | mrn | Sats. aft | aft | aft | aft | aft | Sats. aft | Sats. ngt. | | | | Sundays. mrn | mrn | aft | aft | aft |
|---|---|---|---|---|---|---|---|---|---|---|---|---|---|---|---|---|---|---|---|---|
| | **Andover** Junction.dep. | 8 20 | 8 50 | .... | 1155 | 2 5 | 2 34 | 4 5 | 5 0 | 7 55 | 1020 | .... | .... | .... | .... | .... | 1130 | .... | 6 30 | 8 25 |
| 3½ | Weyhill ............ | 8 27 | .... | .... | 12 3 | 2 12 | .... | 4 13 | 5 8 | 8 3 | 1027 | .... | .... | .... | .... | .... | 1139 | .... | .... | 8 35 |
| 7¼ | Ludgershall ...... arr. | 8 35 | 9 3 | .... | 1210 | 2 19 | 2 44 | 4 21 | 5 15 | 8 10 | 1034 | .... | .... | .... | .... | .... | 1147 | .... | 6 42 | 8 44 |
| | dep. | 8 37 | 9 6 | 1015 | 1229 | 2 20 | 2 47 | 4 22 | 5 20 | 8 15 | 1037 | 12 8 | .... | .... | .... | 9 5 | 1155 | 3 44 | 6 43 | 8 54 |
| 9¾ | **Tidworth** ..........arr. | 8 43 | 9 12 | 1021 | 1235 | 2 26 | 2 53 | 4 28 | 5 26 | 8 21 | 1043 | 1215 | .... | .... | .... | 9 11 | 12 1 | 3 50 | 6 49 | 9 0 |

Bradshaw's Timetable for 1899.

# Chapter Two
## Subsequent History (1891–1923)

The completion of the Cheltenham Extension line can be seen as a turning-point in Midland & South Western Junction history, but this important event was soon followed by another development of equal significance. The M&SWJ company had hitherto suffered from ineffective management and a high turnover of senior officers; in the first few years, for example, control had passed through the hands of T. Harrison Smith (Traffic Manager 1881–1892), B. L. Fearnley (General Manager 1884–1885), and J. F. R. Daniel (General Manager 1885–1892), while C. L. Brooke and A. F. R. Daniel had served as Secretaries for the periods 1873–1885 and 1885–1892 respectively. None of these officers had been able to arrest the steady decline of the railway, but the Midland & South Western Junction company ultimately obtained the services of a first class railway manager.

### The Appointment of Sam Fay

At the end of 1891 the Midland & South Western Directors approached the L&SWR General Manager for advice on the future management of their railway, and as a result they secured the services of Sam Fay (1856–1953), who was seconded from his duties on the South Western to become General Manager and Secretary of the M&SWJR from 1st February, 1892. The existing senior officers were dismissed in one clean sweep, the only survivor being Mr. J. R. Shopland, who retained his position as Engineer.

In the following year, Lt-Colonel F. D. Grey, a Director who had been appointed Receiver in 1884, and whose relations with the rest of the Board were far from amicable, was manoeuvred out of office, and Fay took his place as Receiver, thereby gathering all the reins of control into his capable hands. Sam Fay (later to become well known as Sir Sam Fay, General Manager of the Great Central Railway) was a great and imaginative railway-man if ever there was one. From his correspondence and speeches it is possible to gain a vivid impression of his forceful character and utter devotion to the interests of the struggling company which he had been called upon to serve.

It had indeed, as contemporary accounts show, reached the depths. The fences were broken down, the rolling stock and stations were ill-kempt and dilapidated, and the track was grass-grown. Financially, it could not even make ends meet on revenue account, let alone provide any return on the £1,300,000 capital expenditure. Fay recalled in later years that, when he first went to the M&SWJ he had to wait until the cash takings came in from the stations before he could pay the staff.

Yet despite all the initial difficulties, the financial restrictions imposed by the receivership, and very inadequate engines and rolling stock, after five years of Fay's management the traffic receipts had risen by 63 per cent, with an increase of only 15 per cent in working expenses, and under the M&SWJ Act, 1897, the company was able to effect a settlement with its creditors and obtain a discharge from receivership on 10th November, 1897.

These promising developments were, unfortunately, greatly hampered by the cost and difficulty of working over the antipathetic Great Western — especially on the section between Marlborough Junction and Wolfhall Junction. In the words of Sam Fay, 'it was impossible to get trains of ordinary weight' over the steeply graded single line between Marlborough and Savernake, which the GWR continued to work as one section with wooden staff and ticket until 1893, when electric train staff apparatus was installed. Delays to southbound trains from the M&SWJ at Marlborough South Junction signal box became notorious. It was not unusual to find, in the staff-and-ticket era of working, that the staff was at the Savernake end of the section, and it was widely believed that the GW signalmen were not above contriving this state of affairs deliberately. Vexatious delays occurred also at Savernake, where ticket inspection was compulsory on all M&SWJ trains booked to stop — a time-wasting operation which could be dragged out interminably by the hostile GW staff.

In fairness to the Great Western, it must be said that the timekeeping of Midland & South Western Junction trains during the late 1880s and early 1890s was so bad that there was no way of knowing when a train would actually turn up at Marlborough or Wolfhall junctions, and in these unhappy circumstances GWR signalmen can be forgiven for giving priority to their own trains!

On top of the operational difficulties involved in working over the Great Western, the M&SWJ had to pay £5000 per annum in respect of tolls and other charges for the 'enjoyment' of facilities between Marlborough and Wolfhall Junction — even though it was not allowed to book locally between Marlborough and Savernake. Thus, if a passenger wanted to travel from Marlborough (M&SWJ) to Savernake he had to book to Grafton, and vice versa from Savernake to Ogbourne. The GWR even tried on one occasion to extract a fare from a Midland & South Western Junction General Manager when he was travelling on the footplate of one of his company's engines between Marlborough and Savernake! Moreover, possession of this vital piece of line gave the GWR a stranglehold on the rates charged by the M&SWJ. To quote Fay again, the GWR could 'veto rates for traffic of any description from or to any place, which the managers of other companies and myself may consider fair and reasonable'.

### The Savernake Bottleneck

All this added up to a formidable case for an independent line between Marlborough and Wolfhall, or at the very least for some widening and improvements on the Marlborough branch; but attempts to achieve this in 1884 and 1889 made little headway in the face of Great Western opposition. A further barrier confronting an independent line — the ideal solution — was Savernake Forest, with the problem of squeezing a new railway into the relatively narrow corridor between the forest boundary and the existing Great Western line.

In 1894 the Midland & South Western Junction Board decided to end the Savernake bottleneck once and for all and a committee was appointed to draw up plans for an independent M&SWJ line between Marlborough and

Grafton. This committee worked in close consultation with the Marquess of Ailesbury, the owner of Savernake Forest (and much of the adjoining land) and himself a substantial M&SWJ shareholder. From this there emerged a Bill to incorporate a separate company, called the Marlborough & Grafton Railway, with a share capital of £100,000, borrowing powers of £33,000, and authority to build an entirely new line 5¾ miles long, on a ruling gradient of 1 in 100, from Marlborough to Wolfhall, and to double the existing line for a further mile into Grafton station. The whole scheme was very well prepared. The well-tried technique of creating a separate company was adopted, as the M&SWJ was still in the hands of a Receiver and would have had great difficulty in obtaining the requisite powers or capital in its own name.

The promoters secured from Lord Ailesbury not only his consent to a route which encroached slightly upon the forest, but also the whole of the land needed for the new railway, subject to a rent-charge of £450 per annum and an undertaking to provide a station at Savernake 'adjacent to and at least equal to the existing station of the Great Western Railway Company'. They secured also some strong financial backing, a well-known firm (Messrs John Aird & Sons) to construct the line, and the valuable support of the War Department, which was planning to build extensive barracks at Tidworth and Ludgershall.

Against this array, the opposition of the GWR was fierce but unavailing. The Marlborough & Grafton Bill was passed on 7th August, 1896, and in less than two years the railway was open as a double line throughout. Its chief engineering work was Marlborough tunnel (647 yds), which was driven through the chalk and approached by steep-sided cuttings 70 ft deep at the tunnel entrances. Over the southern portal an inscribed keystone with the heading 'M&GRly 1898' was laid by the Marchioness of Ailesbury at an inaugural ceremony on 2nd July, 1898, though the line had then been open for several days. The existing service was diverted to it on 26th June, 1898, and an improved service started on 1st July, 1898 when the M&SWJ formally took over the railway as tenants.

The M&GR was finally vested in the M&SWJ with effect from 1st August, 1899 under the M&SWJ Act of that date, section 8 of which made binding upon the company the obligation to maintain a separate station at Savernake and stop certain trains there in accordance with the agreement with the Marquess of Ailesbury.

### The Tidworth Line

The last, and most profitable, addition to the Midland & South Western Junction system was not the company's property at all. This was the Tidworth Camp Railway, a branch from Ludgershall to Tidworth, built by War Department contractors, originally as a military siding, subject to an agreement with the M&SWJ dated 19th November, 1900. Under the stress of the South African War (1899–1902) the branch came into use during 1901 for the conveyance of military personnel, stores, and workmen engaged upon the building of Tidworth barracks, under an interim agreement with the M&SWJ company. Its status as a public railway was governed by a subsequent agreement dated 16th February, 1903, whereby the Midland & South Western Junction Railway undertook to man, equip, work and maintain the Tidworth Camp Railway for public traffic on payment to the War Department of an annual rent reckoned at 3 per cent on the capital outlay. The rent was equivalent to £1437 per annum, and the agreement was for an initial term of fourteen years — it was however renewed at the end of that period.

The branch was opened for public goods traffic on 1st July, 1902 and for passengers on 1st October, 1902, and to all outward appearances it formed an integral part of the M&SWJ, though it remained the property of the War Department. It developed such a large volume of traffic that Tidworth became the 'senior' station on the M&SWJ with annual receipts exceeding the total of all other stations on the system put together. The section open for public traffic was 2 miles 33 chains in length and was single track except for nearly ½ mile from the junction at Ludgershall to Perham signal box.

## The Stone Point Railway and Other Abortive Schemes

The Midland & South Western Junction Railway was associated with several abortive schemes, and some of these interesting projects are worthy of mention.

The 'Solent scheme', or Stone Point Railway, was in part an attempt to carry out the third stage of the original plan of 1872, namely, to reach the coast beyond Fawley, though it was also regarded by the Midland & South Western Junction as a peg on which to hang its claim to the valuable running powers over the L&SWR from Andover to Southampton. As already recorded, these powers were granted by the Swindon Marlborough & Andover Act of 1882, which authorised also a line 12 miles 49 chains in length from the L&SWR at Totton to a termination on the foreshore of the Solent at Stone Point, opposite Cowes, together with a west curve at Redbridge Junction; a further SM&A Act in 1883 authorised the construction of a deep-water pier 470 yds long at Stone Point. No capital was raised or work started on any of these projects, the powers for which were transferred to a new company, called the South Hampshire Railway & Pier Company, incorporated by Act of 25th June, 1886, with additional authority to build a hotel at Fawley.

Subsequent Acts in the name of this company kept the original 'Solent scheme' alive until its abandonment in 1893, by which time the Cheltenham Extension was open and the M&SWJ had started to exercise its running powers into Southampton. In 1903 the London & South Western Railway itself obtained powers for a light railway from Totton to Fawley, but there was no attempt to begin construction and World War I intervened before further progress could be made. Finally, in 1921 'The Totton Hythe & Fawley Light Railway Company' was formed to build a standard gauge branch along the edge of Southampton Water to Fawley; the proposed line — which can be seen as a lineal descendent of the original 'Solent Scheme' — would have been 9 miles 1 chain long (slightly shorter than the present Fawley branch), and the estimated cost was £252,327. In 1923 the Totton &

Fawley powers were taken over by the newly-created Southern Railway, and the branch was belatedly opened under SR auspices on 20th July, 1925, some fifty years after the Solent Scheme had first been mooted!

The Collingbourne & Avon Valley Railway, incorporated on 7th August, 1888, had power to build a line of 7 miles 26 chains from the M&SWJ south of Collingbourne station westward to Netheravon, where one of the promoters, Sir Michael Hicks-Beach, Bart., owned property. The line was planned as a light railway with gradients of 1 in 50. Schemes to provide the Avon valley with rail communication were as numerous as they were unsuccessful, and in 1888 a Pewsey & Salisbury Railway, authorised in 1883, was still nominally alive, though no construction was ever started. It was formally abandoned in 1891, and the Collingbourne scheme likewise foundered.

It is interesting to note that Sir Michael Hicks-Beach (later Lord St Aldwyn) had interests in other local railways, including the East Gloucestershire and of course the M&SWJ itself. An eminent Tory politician, Sir Michael achieved high office under both Disraeli and Lord Salisbury, and he was (at various times) Chief Secretary for Ireland, Leader of the House and Chancellor of the Exchequer. The support of such a well-known figure must have helped struggling local companies such as the M&SWJ in their dealings with the Great Western!

Mention of the East Gloucestershire Railway is a reminder that a branch from Cirencester to an end-on junction with the EGR at Fairford had been authorised by the Swindon & Cheltenham Extension Act of 1881, and the prospect of such a line being built seemed, at first, to be promising. The first mile of the proposed Fairford line was indicated by the eastward trend of the main line as it left Cirencester for the north, but further progress was halted by the financial crisis of 1884. It was formally abandoned under the M&SWJ Act, 1889, wherein the company was pledged not to oppose the construction of a similar branch by the East Gloucestershire Railway 'or persons acting on its behalf' — presumably the GWR. The latter made no move to construct anything of the sort, and a local attempt in 1901 to launch the 'Fairford & Cirencester Railway' came to nothing.

Meanwhile, the passing of the Locomotives on Highways Act, 1896, which eased the restrictions on the use of mechanically propelled vehicles on roads, prompted the idea of running a 'road train' between Cirencester and Fairford in connection with the M&SWJ and GWR. The result was the appearance in 1897 of a quaint contraption consisting of a steam-driven motor van, designed to carry 2½ to 3 tons of goods or luggage, coupled to a trailer capable of seating 20 passengers. The power unit located beneath the body of the van, comprised an oil-fired boiler supplying steam at 225 lb. per square inch pressure to a double-tandem compound engine, with gear transmission to the driving wheels. Its rated maximum speed was 8 mph, but the working speed was limited to 6 mph. The vehicle was not railway owned or operated but ran as an experimental and short-lived private venture.

## Looking Further North

In the north, where dependence upon the Great Western line between Andoversford Junction and Lansdown Junction, Cheltenham, produced the same difficulties and delays as had occurred between Marlborough and Grafton, the M&SWJ launched two ambitious projects, which, though unsuccessful in themselves, brought lasting benefit to the company. The first was the Andoversford & Stratford-upon-Avon Railway, for which a Bill was promoted in the session of 1898 with the object of building a railway, 25 miles 70 chains in length, from a junction with the M&SWJ north of Dowdeswell station via Winchcombe and Broadway to a junction with the Birmingham, North Warwickshire & Stratford-upon-Avon Railway at Stratford. This company had been incorporated in 1894 to build a line from an independent station in Birmingham to Stratford, but in 1898 the scheme was still in abeyance, though at one time the Great Central Railway had cast eyes on it as offering means of access to Birmingham. The M&SWJ now came forward with an agreement to work the North Warwickshire when opened, and the Andoversford company was promoted to form the necessary link, which was to be double line throughout.

The Andoversford & Stratford-upon-Avon Bill passed successfully through the Commons but was defeated in the House of Lords when the Great Western gave a formal pledge to construct a line from Cheltenham to Honeybourne, connecting there with the existing branch to Stratford-upon-Avon. (The Honeybourne line was eventually completed in 1906.)

In 1899 the M&SWJ tried again, this time with the Midland & South Western Junction Railway Northern Extension Bill, in which powers were sought for a 14 mile line from Andoversford via Winchcombe to a junction with the Midland Railway just south of Ashchurch station. This move led to negotiations between the M&SWJ, the Midland, and the GWR, and to two important agreements, which did much to settle the future relationships and fortunes of the Midland & South Western Junction Railway.

Under the first agreement (14th March, 1899), to which all three companies were parties, the Bill for the Ashchurch line was withdrawn, and the M&SWJ secured freedom to fix through rates and fares in respect of traffic carried over the GWR line between Andoversford Junction and Lansdown Junction without interference from the Great Western as though the Ashchurch line had been built. The GWR undertook to double the Lansdown Junction to Andoversford Junction line, in return for a similar undertaking that the M&SWJ would continue the widening southward to Cirencester.

The second agreement (10th April, 1899), scheduled to the Midland Railway Act, 1899, concerned the M&SWJ and the Midland only and had as its stated object 'that a permanent alliance should be established between the two companies'. Under its terms, the Midland agreed to give preference to the M&SWJ route for through traffic from places both south and west of Derby to places on the L&SWR bounded by Lymington, Andover, and Portsmouth, including Southampton. The Midland received running powers over the GWR from Cheltenham to Andoversford Junction and over the whole of the M&SWJ and agreed to lend £200,000 to the M&SWJ over a period of four years for the improvement and development of the line for through traffic. The loan was granted on easy terms imposing no immediate obligation on the M&SWJ to pay interest; it was increased to £250,000 by a supplementary agreement in 1902.

The agreements of 1899 marked the climax of Fay's term of office as General Manager, which he vacated in April 1899 on his return to the L&SWR as superintendent of the line. In seven years he had rescued the M&SWJ company from bankruptcy, freed it from Great Western domination, and set it on the road to the further development of its line and traffic. His successors as General Managers of the company were James Purkess (in office 1899–1902), who came from the L&SWR, and John Davies (1903–23), who had been General Manager of the Government Railways of Western Australia. The former cashier, E. T. Lawrence, succeeded Fay as Secretary; he was followed, on his appointment in 1908 to Secretaryship of the Barry Railway, by S. H. Webber, who held office until 1917, when the post was again combined with that of the General Manager.

The doubling of the M&SWJ made possible by the Midland loan, was confined to each end of the system and was completed in stages, namely, Andoversford to Withington (2nd September, 1900), Cirencester to Foss Cross (12th July, 1901), and Foss Cross to Withington (8th June, 1902). With the GW section from Andoversford Junction to Lansdown Junction (completed on 28th September, 1902), M&SWJ trains thus had a run of 21 miles on double track between Cirencester and Cheltenham. At the southern end, the stages were Weyhill to Ludgershall (28th August, 1900), Ludgershall to Collingbourne (1st September, 1901), and Collingbourne to Grafton (2nd November, 1902). With the Marlborough & Grafton line, already double, this gave a continuous stretch of 17¾ miles.

The section from Weyhill to Andover Junction had perforce to remain single, as the M&SWJ was debarred by the agreement of 1873 from making a connection with the L&SWR at Red Post Junction, but it had the exclusive use of the separate third road into Andover Junction station. This prohibition was set aside under the stress of war. In 1917 a crossing loop and connection were put in at Red Post Junction; these survived until 1936. In 1943 the line was doubled from Weyhill to Red Post Junction, where a permanent connection and signal box were opened. It remained, however, a normal practice for most regular passenger trains on the M&SWJ route to run over the third road, which was signalled for operation as a single line tablet section between Red Post Junction box and Andover Junction West box.

In its final form, the M&SWJ owned 60 miles 55 chains of railway (route mileage), including the connections to the GWR at Rushey Platt and Wolfhall, and worked 2 miles 33 chains (the Tidworth Camp Railway). In addition, it exercised statutory running powers totalling 37 miles 22 chains over the lines of other companies, namely, 29 miles 28 chains over the L&SWR from Red Post Junction to Southampton, 6 miles 72 chains over the GWR from Andoversford Junction to Lansdown Junction, and 1 mile 2 chains over the Midland from Lansdown Junction to Cheltenham (High Street).

A fine view of MSWJ locomotive No. 6 at Eastleigh on 14th April, 1922.

H.C. Casserley

# Chapter Three
## Operating the M&SWJR

Midland & South Western Junction train services were never intensive, and for the first ten years the M&SWJR timetable was entirely local in character. South of Swindon five or six trains on weekdays (and two on Sundays) formed the average service, while two on weekdays only were the normal quota between Swindon and Cirencester.

The timetable arrangements for the full opening of the Cheltenham Extension on 1st August, 1891 were chaotic. The Directors had planned, and even announced locally, a service of five through trains (one of them 'fast') between Andover and Cheltenham, but it is unlikely that more than three of them ever ran, and those certainly not to time. Amusingly, when Fay took charge in 1892 and insisted upon punctuality, he was reported to have received a crop of complaints from people up and down the line who had missed trains — so engrained had become the habit of arriving to catch a train on the M&SWJ 15 or 20 minutes *after* the advertised time of departure!

An improved service was put on in the summer of 1892 with the aid of two engines and sets of coaches borrowed from the L&SWR, which worked between Southampton and Cheltenham from 1st May, 1892. In the following year a through coach ran between Sheffield and Southampton, starting on 1st July, 1893 and continuing until the end of October. This service reappeared on 1st June, 1894, when the train was worked by M&SWJ engines and crews throughout between Cheltenham and Southampton. It was the forerunner of the famous 'North' and 'South' Expresses, the crack trains on the M&SWJ, which reached their zenith in the decade before World War I, and for all too short a period gave a really creditable cross-country service between Southampton and the north. The best scheduled times during that period over the 94¾ miles between Southampton West (now Central) and Cheltenham were 2 hours 27 minutes northbound and 2 hours 36 minutes southbound.

Except for a short-lived through train between Portsmouth and Cheltenham in the summer of 1898, the southern terminal for these through coaches was Southampton, but the northern terminals varied, ranging from Manchester to Leeds and Bradford, and there were occasional inconsistencies. For example, in some years coaches ran southbound from Manchester Central (Midland) but returned northbound to Sheffield. From 1st May, 1911 the Manchester through coach ran to and from London Road (L&NWR) via Crewe and Birmingham New Street, where transfer to and from the Midland took place. The morning South Express and the afternoon North Express carried through coaches between Southampton and Birmingham (sometimes Derby). Through coaches to and from the more northerly points were conveyed over the M&SWJ on the morning North Express and afternoon South Express.

At the peak of the M&SWJ passenger services in 1913 there were six through trains on weekdays from Cheltenham to Andover, with one 'short' train from Cheltenham to Swindon and two from Swindon to Andover; in the northbound direction there were seven through trains from Andover to

# GOODS TRAFFIC.

## MIDLAND & SOUTH WESTERN JUNC. RLY. Co.,

### GENERAL CARRIERS

#### TO AND FROM ALL PARTS OF

# ENGLAND AND SCOTLAND.

THE MIDLAND & SOUTH WESTERN JUNCTION COMPANY HAVE THROUGH BOOKING ARRANGE-MENTS FOR GOODS TRAFFIC, AND CARRYING CONNECTIONS BY A SERVICE OF EXPRESS TRAINS BETWEEN LONDON, THE SOUTH OF ENGLAND, BRISTOL, THE MIDLANDS, AND NORTH OF ENGLAND, AND ALL STATIONS ON THE COMPANY'S LINE OF RAILWAY.

A service of Express Goods Trains has also been established between Manchester, Birmingham, Wolverhampton, Nottingham, Leeds and Bradford, and stations on the Midland Company's system generally and SOUTHAMPTON DOCKS, to and from which the Company's trains run direct.   Goods leaving Manchester and other large trade centres in the North by Midland route in the evening reach Southampton in time for shipment the following morning.

THE SOUTHAMPTON DOCKS, owned by the London and South Western Railway Company, are situated within a very sheltered harbour, and have the natural advantage of double tides, with four hours of high water every tide, affording unrivalled accommodation for THE LARGEST STEAM SHIPS AFLOAT, at any time of the day or night.

THE EMPRESS DOCK is an open dock, 18½ acres in extent, with a minimum water depth of 26 feet at low water of spring tides, and an entrance 165 feet wide ; its quays measure 3,750 lineal feet.  The new Quay extensions in the Rivers Itchen and Test are now open and measure 4,000 lineal feet.  In addition there is an Open Dock of 16 acres, entrance 150 feet wide, with a depth of about 31 feet at high water spring tides and 27 feet at neap tides, also a Close Dock of 10 acres approached from the Open Dock.  In all there are 19,000 lineal feet of Quay accommodation, with Warehouses and Cargo Sheds adjacent.

There are SIX LARGE DRY DOCKS with all necessary appurtenances, where the largest vessels can be dealt with Trafalgar Dock being the DEEPEST GRAVING DOCK IN THE WORLD.

There is a complete system of Railways of 34 miles, extending to all Quays, and into and alongside each Warehouse, worked by Locomotive Engines.  The Midland and South Western Junction Railway Trucks pass direct between the Docks and the Midlands and North of England.

IMPORT AND EXPORT CARGO.—Cargoes of every description are landed and warehoused, or forwarded by railway with great expedition.   There are extensive BONDED AND FREE WAREHOUSES on the Dock Quays for COCOA, COFFEE, TEA, TOBACCO, CIGARS, and every description of Merchandise ; also Large Vaults for Wines and Spirits under Bond and Bottling facilities.

For the Provision, Fruit, and Potato Trades, every facility exists, and dispatch to the Midlands and the Northern Markets made immediately after landing.

The largest installation of Cold Storage in Europe is now in operation for the direct Import of Meat and Produce, Ships being able to discharge right alongside, with a depth of water of 32 feet L.W.O.S.T.

There is a complete system of Steam, Hydraulic and Electric Power (Sheers, Cranes, Hoists, Elevators, Capstans, &c.. &c.), with lifting power varying from one to fifty tons ; and also Steam Sheers to lift up to eighty tons.  The whole of the Dock Quays, Sheds and approaches are lighted by Electricity.

Fish traffic from Hull, Grimsby, and the East Coast is conveyed by Express Trains and promptly delivered at Cirencester, Swindon, Marlborough, Andover, and Southampton.

The Midland and South Western Junction Railway Company have through booking arrangements for Fruit and Vegetable and Potato Traffic, from the Channel Islands and French Ports, to Gloucester, Birmingham, Manchester, and the North of England generally, which, in conjunction with the South Western fast Steamers, and the Midland Company's Express Trains from Cheltenham, is conveyed and delivered with the utmost despatch.

Goods and Parcels from LONDON AND THE SOUTH AND WEST OF ENGLAND FOR MARLBOROUGH, SWINDON, CIRENCESTER, CHELTENHAM, and other M. & S.W.J.R. Stations should be addressed " PER SOUTH WESTERN RAILWAY, via ANDOVER " and goods from MANCHESTER, THE NORTH OF ENGLAND, BIRMINGHAM, WORCESTER, GLOUCESTER, BRISTOL, &c., should be addressed " PER MIDLAND RAILWAY, via CHELTENHAM."   Traffic from SOUTHAMPTON TO THE MIDLANDS AND THE NORTH should be addressed " via ANDOVER JUNCTION."

Rates and other information may be obtained on application to MR. J. M. MALERBI, the Company's District Traffic Superintendent, 2 Cook's Buildings, Oxford Street, Southampton.

Extract from the July 1915  MSWJ timetable.

Cheltenham. The Sunday service included two through trains southbound and three northbound.

The afternoon North Express was allowed 105 minutes for the 68½ miles from Andover to Cheltenham with a stop at Swindon only, but the highest speeds were probably achieved by the afternoon South Express, which was allowed 31 minutes for the 21½ miles from Marlborough to Andover, including a two-minute stop at Ludgershall. These fast workings did not carry milk or horse-box traffic, but they were apt to suffer delays on the single line sections between Cirencester and Marlborough and so had to make up time on the double line stretches to ensure connections at Andover and Cheltenham.

Another interesting train was the 'American and Cape Lines Boat Express' which left Cheltenham at about 5 am on one morning in the week (occasionally two) with through coaches from Bradford to Southampton Docks. It originated in July 1893 and was run for the benefit mainly of emigrants wishing to join ocean liners at Southampton. It was an early casualty in World War I when M&SWJ services were drastically curtailed, never again to recover their former brilliance. The afternoon North Express vanished permanently, but a through service between Southampton and Manchester (London Road), restored in the summer of 1921, was diverted to Liverpool (Lime Street) in the autumn of that year and in this form continued until the outbreak of World War II in September 1939.

The list of through bookings available from M&SWJ stations via Cheltenham or Andover was extensive, ranging from Edinburgh in the north to Paris in the south; from Marlborough one could book through to Brecon in one direction and to Newmarket in the other — the latter for the benefit of the racing fraternity. Inwards there were through bookings from Waterloo to all M&SWJ stations, including Cheltenham, which at one time could be reached in 3 hours 19 minutes from Waterloo, with a change at Andover Junction. Tickets were white for first class, blue for second, and pink for third; second class bookings were abolished on 1st January, 1904.

Passenger train receipts, including milk and parcels, accounted for about half of the Midland & South Western Junction Railway's gross revenue, and in 1913 — a good year — passenger traffic reached 54 per cent of the total revenue.

## Freight Traffic

The M&SWJR also competed energetically for goods traffic, especially through traffic destined for Southampton Docks, though until the agreement of 1899 it was hampered by the ability of the GWR to interfere with rates and charges. Yet through traffic was secured from the earliest days, for example, coal from South Wales and the Forest of Dean via Rushey Platt to the L&SWR, and even (at a later date) bricks from Bristol to Marlborough via the Midland Railway and Cheltenham.

The company looked northwards for its most important source of through traffic, and an early contribution to the flow (in an almost literal sense!) was 'Burton Beer for export, and for Portsmouth', which was carried over the

## MIDLAND AND SOUTH WESTERN JUNCTION RAILWAY.

### THE COMPANY HAVE ARRANGED THE FOLLOWING

# REDUCED Scale of Rates for Farm and Dairy Produce

by GOODS Trains between M. & S.W. Jnc. Stations and London (Nine Elms).
Delivered to the Markets in London or within the ordinary limits.

| STATIONS. | Fresh Meat, Dead Poultry, Dead Rabbits. | | | | * Eggs, Butter, Fruit. | | | | Apples and Pears Packed. | | | |
|---|---|---|---|---|---|---|---|---|---|---|---|---|
| | Any Quantity Small as per Scale. | One Ton Lots. | Two Ton Lots. | Three Ton Lots. | Any Q'nty. Small as per Scale. | One Ton Lots. | Two Ton Lots. | Three Ton Lots. | Any Q'nty. Small as per Scale. | One Ton Lots. | Two Ton Lots. | Three Ton Lots. |
| ANDOVER JUNCTION ... | 26/- | 24/3 | 23/- | 22/6 | 18/2 | 17/4 | 16/6 | 15/7 | 14/9 | 13/10 | 13/5 | 13/- |
| WEYHILL ... ... | 26/10 | 25/2 | 23/- | 22/6 | 19/1 | 17/9 | 16/11 | 16/- | 15/2 | 14/4 | 13/10 | 13/5 |
| LUDGERSHALL ... ... | 26/10 | 25/2 | 23/10 | 23/- | 19/1 | 17/9 | 16/11 | 16/- | 15/2 | 14/4 | 13/10 | 13/5 |
| TIDWORTH ... ... | 27/11 | 26/2 | 24/10 | 24/- | 20/1 | 18/10 | 17/11 | 17/1 | 16/2 | 15/4 | 14/11 | 14/6 |
| COLLINGBOURNE ... | 26/10 | 25/2 | 23/10 | 23/- | 19/1 | 17/9 | 16/11 | 16/- | 15/2 | 14/4 | 13/10 | 13/5 |
| GRAFTON ... ... | | | | | | | | | | | | |
| SAVERNAKE ... ... | | | | | | | | | | | | |
| MARLBOROUGH ... ... | 27/9 | 26/- | 24/8 | 23/5 | 19/11 | 18/8 | 17/4 | 16/6 | 15/7 | 14/9 | 14/4 | 13/10 |
| OGBOURNE ... ... | 28/7 | 26/10 | 25/7 | 23/10 | 20/10 | 19/8 | 18/2 | 17/4 | 16/- | 15/2 | 14/9 | 14/4 |
| CHISELDON ... ... | | | | | | | | | | | | |
| SWINDON ... ... | 27/9 | 26/- | 24/8 | 23/5 | 19/11 | 18/8 | 17/4 | 16/6 | 15/7 | 14/9 | 14/4 | 13/10 |
| RUSHEY PLATT ... ... | | | | | | | | | | | | |
| BLUNSDON ... ... | 28/7 | 26/10 | 25/7 | 23/10 | 20/10 | 19/8 | 18/2 | 17/4 | 16/- | 15/2 | 14/9 | 14/4 |
| CRICKLADE ... ... | | | | | | | | | | | | |
| CERNEY ... ... | 29/6 | 27/9 | 26/- | 24/3 | 21/8 | 20/4 | 19/1 | 18/2 | 16/6 | 15/7 | 15/2 | 14/9 |
| CIRENCESTER ... ... | 30/4 | 28/7 | 26/5 | 24/8 | 22/6 | 21/3 | 19/11 | 19/1 | 16/11 | 16/- | 15/7 | 15/2 |
| FOSS CROSS ... ... | 31/2 | 29/- | 26/10 | 25/2 | 23/5 | 22/1 | 20/10 | 19/6 | 17/4 | 16/6 | 16/- | 15/7 |
| WITHINGTON ... ... | 32/11 | 30/4 | 28/2 | 26/- | 24/8 | 23/- | 21/8 | 20/4 | 18/2 | 17/4 | 16/6 | 16/- |
| DOWDESWELL ... ... | | | | | | | | | | | | |
| CHELTENHAM .. ... | 38/10 | 34/8 | 29/6 | 26/10 | 27/10 24/8 { For lots not less than 10 cwt. | 23/- | 21/8 | 20/4 | 18/2 | 17/4 | 16/6 | 16/- |

* Eggs in Boxes, Cases or Crates at Owner's Risk.
Butter in Casks, Firkins, Baskets, Flats and Hampers with lids, or Boxes, or in Tubs or Cools with wooden lids.
Fruit (not hothouse), viz. :—Cherries, Raspberries and Strawberries in Tubs for Jam making, Blackberries, Cranberries, Currants (not Grocers'), Damsons, Gooseberries, Greengages, Medlars, Plums, Walnuts and Whortleberries, Tomatoes, except in Baskets without Lids.
If senders require the produce collected at sending station, the rate for Fresh Meat, Dead Poultry and Dead Rabbits will be *1/8* per ton more than the figures named ; for Eggs, Butter and Fruit, *1/6* per ton more ; and for Apples and Pears packed, *1/4* per ton more.
Full Particulars as to Rates for conveyance by Passenger and Goods Train of all descriptions of Farm and Dairy Produce in large quantities may be obtained from the General Manager.

Extract from the July 1915 MSWJ timetable.

M&SWJ route from 1st June, 1892, as recorded in the Board minutes. Through traffic from the Midland under the 1899 agreement did not develop quite so well as had been expected and this led to a dispute between the two companies, which went to arbitration; but the volume justified the running of regular freight trains by night between Cheltenham and Southampton.

Military traffic both in goods and personnel was all-important. It became a prominent feature during the South African War, at the end of which the company and its officers received a special commendation from the Secretary of State for War, thanking them for their 'untiring and zealous services rendered in connection with the assembling and despatch of troops to the seat of war'. This achievement was totally eclipsed in World War I when the M&SWJ ran 6452 special troop trains and 1488 ambulance trains, and carried nearly 3,200,000 officers and men and 135,000 horses, as well as large quantities of ammunition and supplies. No one who lived near the M&SWJ in those years will readily forget the crowded trains, the continuous flow of troops and stores, and the fascinating variety of the coaching stock on specials from far afield.

In peace time the Midland & South Western Junction Railway provided many troop specials for the annual manoeuvres on Salisbury Plain and issued an elaborate folder in colours, containing a map of the area with camps and barracks clearly marked, diagrams of Ludgershall and Tidworth stations, a train service summary, and a picture of a mounted cavalryman on the front.

## Profit and Loss

Unfortunately, wartime traffic under conditions of government control brought no additional reward to the shareholders of the M&SWJ, for most of whom the company remained an unprofitable concern until the end of its days. The financial structure was hopelessly top-heavy. The amount of paid-up capital ranking for dividend, including the Midland loan, was approximately £2,124,000, of which nearly £1½ millions, consisting of rent charge stock, loans, and debentures, took precedence over preference capital of £337,000 and ordinary capital totalling less than £292,000. The bulk of the preference and ordinary capital was in small holdings of less than £500 each.

In its best year, 1913, the company had just over £25,000 available for distribution, or less than 1¼ per cent on the whole of the capital; this was sufficient to pay interest in full at 3 per cent per annum on the two top-ranking stocks, ½ per cent on the 'B' Debentures, and over £5,000 towards the service of the Midland loan, but there was nothing for the holders of 'C' Debentures and lower categories of stock totalling £820,000 (nominal). Thus, much of the original capital raised for the construction of the line had been lost, and the holders received derisory amounts* of Great Western deferred certificates (ranking for dividend from 1st January, 1929) when the M&SWJ company was finally absorbed by its mighty neighbour. The Midland loan, which had been drawn on to a total of £244,000, was discharged by the issue of £85,000 Great Western 5 per cent preference stock.

* £4 per £100 (nominal) of the various classes of preference shares and stock, and £2 for each £100 in ordinary shares.

## A Note on Signalling and Trackwork

Permanent way on the Swindon Marlborough & Andover line south of Rushey Platt was laid originally with flat-bottomed rail of Vignoles pattern, manufactured by the German firm of Krupp, in lengths of 18 to 24 feet, weighing 70 lb. per linear yard. The Cheltenham extension, in contrast, had chaired track formed of 75 lb. bullhead section rail in lengths of 21 to 30 feet. Much of this 75 lb. track survived as the down line from Andoversford to Cirencester until 1928. Elsewhere the old track was gradually replaced in the early part of this century by 87 lb. bullhead rail, which had been laid on the Marlborough & Grafton line.

The signals, and signal boxes and locking gear south of Cirencester were supplied by the Gloucester Wagon Company, a few of whose frames, e.g. at Grafton and Collingbourne, survived for many years. The early signals were of an old-fashioned type fitted with a red spectacle glass only, thus displaying a plain white light when 'off'; some of them remained in use between Cricklade and Marlborough until 1904.

The single line sections of the M&SWJ were worked on Tyer's electric tablet system in accordance with an undertaking given to the Board of Trade in 1891. As already mentioned, the Cheltenham Extension north of Cirencester was worked on this system from the date of opening in 1891, and within a short time it had replaced the staff-and-ticket method on the older parts of the line.

Between Marlborough and Grafton — the first double line length of any consequence on the M&SWJ — Sykes lock-and-block apparatus was installed for the opening in 1898, but the volume of traffic was found not to justify this method, so it was replaced in 1902 by Tyer's three-position single wire block indicators, which had been adopted on the recently widened sections at each end of the system.

Locking frames built by the firm of W. R. Sykes were installed at Rushey Platt, Swindon, and Wolfhall Junction when the boxes were rebuilt in 1905. The signals supplied for this new work and for replacements generally throughout the system were of a type designed by Evans, O'Donnell & Co., much favoured by the L&SWR at one time. The M&SWJ had a very good record for safety, and its career was not marred by any serious accident.

## The Locomotive Stock

If the signalling equipment of the L&SWR had something in common with that of the M&SWJ, the locomotive policy in later years followed that of the Midland with the adoption of 0−6−0 and 4−4−0 tender engines as standard for the line. This, however, was after the M&SWJ had already acquired an interesting assortment of other types. In all, 38 locomotives passed through its ownership (including those purchased by the SM&A), but the stock at any one time never exceeded 31 engines.

For the opening from Swindon to Marlborough in 1881, the SM&A procured from Dübs & Co. three small 0−6−0 side-tank engines, with outside cylinders and 4 ft driving wheels, numbered 1−3 and intended primarily for goods traffic. For passenger work, three 2−4−0 side-tank engines were obtained from Beyer, Peacock & Co. in 1882, and a fourth, which was slightly larger, was added in 1884; they were numbered 5–8. They had inside cylinders and 5 ft 6 in. driving wheels, and appear to have been very useful engines, more so than the Dübs 0–6–0s which proved to have a rather limited range of use because of their small driving wheels.

The Swindon & Cheltenham Extension Railway did not work its own traffic or possess any locomotives, and so the opening stock of the M&SWJ when it was formed by amalgamation in 1884 comprised these seven tank engines, plus a freak which, in the event, contributed next to nothing to the motive power of the company. This was SM&A No. 4, an 0–4–4 side-tank with outside cylinders, built by the Avonside Engine Co., of Bristol, for the Fairlie Engine Co., of Westminster, and exhibited at the Paris Exhibition of 1878. It was a single-boiler, double-bogie Fairlie type, the leading (steam-driven) bogie under the smoke box having wheels of 5 ft 6 in. diameter, and the trailing bogie 4 ft wheels. It was moreover one of the first locomotives in this country to be fitted with the Walschaerts valve motion. No. 4 came first to the Swindon Marlborough & Andover on loan, but in March 1882 the Directors decided to buy it outright for £1,000. It was not a good bargain. No doubt No. 4 looked large and powerful in comparison with the other tank engines on the line, and this may account for the nickname 'Jumbo' which it seems to have acquired; it certainly was not derived from elephantine qualities of haulage power or longevity. Large bills for repairs soon came in, and in 1884 the locomotive foreman reported:

> No. 4 is little or no use to us for train work, as she can never be depended on and is the most expensive engine we have for working.

Sam Fay made short work of the unfortunate 'Jumbo' when he arrived in 1892, and it was scrapped early in that year, though there were left only the original seven engines to provide motive power for a line now grown to nearly 70 miles in length. Nor was any money available for the purchase of additions; indeed the company still owed over £11,000 for stock delivered nearly ten years earlier.

### Mortgaging the Rolling Stock

In 1893 one of the Directors, Percy Mortimer, came to the company's rescue with a personal advance of £2360 for the purchase of a 4–4–0 tender engine (No. 9) built by Dübs & Co., with inside cylinders and 6 ft driving wheels; in the original form it had a stovepipe chimney. In the following year Sam Fay secured the consent of the Court of Chancery to establish a rolling stock trust fund (amounting eventually to £70,000) with Sir Charles Scotter, General Manager of the L&SWR, and Sir Michael Hicks-Beach as trustees, and in this way the M&SWJ was able to borrow money on security of the stock purchased. Another object of the trust was to defray the cost of repair shops at Cirencester, which came into use in 1895 — hitherto the company had sent its engines at great expense to London for heavy repairs.

Experience with No. 9 seems to have shown that the track was not yet in a condition to carry in safety a 4–4–0 weighing (with tender) 69 tons, and the next three engines were somewhat lighter 2-4-0s with 5 ft 6 in. coupled wheels and 17 in. × 24 in. cylinders. Like No. 9 (which they closely resembled), the new 2-4-0s were built by Dübs & Co. of Glasgow; when first delivered they had stovepipe chimneys. The engines were delivered in 1894, and took the numbers 10, 11 and 12. They were, in retrospect, a very successful class and in the end outlived all other engines owned by the M&SWJ. All three passed into the hands of the GWR in 1923 and, after rebuilding, finished their days in the Didcot and Reading areas, sometimes working on the Lambourn branch; No. 12 (GWR No. 1336) survived until 1954.

Two 0-6-0T goods engines completed the batch of locomotives delivered by Dübs & Co. in 1894; one of these was regarded as a replacement for 'Jumbo' and so took the number 4, while its companion became M&SWJ No. 13 (No. 4 was renumbered in 1914 when it became No. 14). The two 0-6-0Ts had 4 ft 7 in. wheels and 17 in. × 24 in. cylinders; their weight in working order was 49 tons, and they carried 1,000 gallons of water.

The company then reverted to Beyer, Peacock and obtained an 0-4-4 side-tank engine (No. 15) with 5 ft 2 in. driving wheels, and two remarkable 2-6-0 tender engines (Nos. 14 and 16). No. 14 had been designed for a South American railway, but proved sufficiently useful on the M&SWJ for the company to order another of the same type. Both engines had 4 ft driving wheels, outside cylinders, and very long frames in proportion to the boiler; in all they had a distinctly 'foreign' appearance. One was stationed at Cheltenham and the other at Andover for the task of hauling the heavy through freight trains between Southampton and Cheltenham, which were such a vital source of revenue for the M&SWJ.

No. 14 was withdrawn in 1914 and sold, without the boiler, to Wakes, of Darlington, in 1918. After rebuilding, it worked at the Cramlington Colliery, Northumberland. No. 16 survived to be taken over by the GWR and worked in the Bristol area until 1930, fitted with a Belpaire boiler.

The last of the miscellaneous types procured by the M&SWJ were two 4-4-4 side-tank engines (Nos. 17 and 18) of a most distinguished and handsome design, built by Sharp, Stewart & Co. for main line passenger work and delivered in 1897; they had inside cylinders and 5 ft 3 in. driving wheels.

The 4-4-4T wheel arrangement was rare in this country, but on the reverse curves of the M&SWJ it had its merits. Nos. 17 and 18 were fast running engines with good acceleration, capable of picking up time on the stopping trains which formed the bulk of the passenger service. In the last year or two of the company's independent existence, one of these engines was often to be seen on the up (northbound) stopping train leaving Andover Junction at 2.40 pm. The appearance of this train, as it emerged at full speed from Marlborough tunnel with No. 17 or 18 at its head and swung round the curve to a smart stop in the station, typified all that had been best in the character and performance of the M&SWJ in its heyday. After grouping No. 18 was fitted with a GWR standard taper boiler and worked in the Kidderminster area for several years.

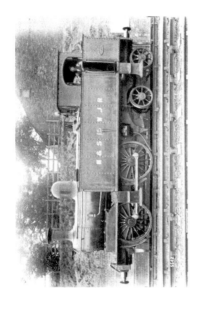

*Top left*: Swindon, Marlborough and Andover Railway 0–6–0T. No. 1 built by Dübs in 1881. *Top right*: Locomotive No. 15, 0–4–4T of the MSWJR built by Beyer Peacock in 1895. *Bottom left*: MSWJ No. 9, 4–4–0 tender locomotive built by Dübs in 1893 and *bottom right*: The unusual looking 2–6–0, No. 16 tender locomotive built by Beyer Peacock in 1897.

R. W. Kidner Collection

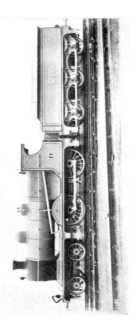

*Top left:* No. 11, 2–4–0 tender locomotive seen here as GWR No. 1335, with its GWR boiler, *Top right:* Seen in MSWJR livery is No. 17, 4–4–4T built by Sharp Stewart in 1897. *Bottom left:* Locomotive No. 4, 4–4–0 tender locomotive built by the North British Co. in 1914 and *bottom right:* MSWJR locomotive No. 3, 4–4–0 tender engine seen here rebuilt as GWR No. 1121.

R.W. Kidner Collection

## A New Locomotive Policy

By 1899, when the M&SWJ possessed 18 locomotives embracing eight different classes from three manufacturers, some attempt at a more settled policy was clearly overdue. Thereafter all additions or replacements were either 0−6−0s or 4−4−0 tender engines.

The 0−6−0s comprised a class of ten engines numbered 19−28, all built by Beyer, Peacock with 5 ft 2½ in. driving wheels and 18 in. × 26 in. inside cylinders; six were delivered in 1899 and the remaining four in 1902. They were very robust and serviceable engines, designed both for goods and passenger work. All of them passed into the ownership of the GWR in 1923 and were eventually rebuilt with conical (taper) boilers, being the first 0−6−0s on the GWR to have this type of boiler until the appearance of the '2251' class in 1930. The last survivor was No. 21 (GWR No. 1005), which was withdrawn in March 1938.

The 4−4−0s were another outstandingly attractive class, and the one by which M&SWJ locomotives are most generally remembered. A total of nine came into service between 1905 and 1914 from the works of the North British Locomotive Co., all with the same general features, though the last two (Nos. 4 and 31) had Ross pop safety valves and a top water-feed device on the boiler, housed in a small separate flat-topped dome surmounted by the safety valves, behind the steam dome which was placed far forward. The coupled wheels were 5 ft 9 in. in diameter, boiler pressure was 160 lb. per square inch, and tractive effort at 75 per cent of working pressure was 14,650 lb. They cost an average of £2800 each.

Conspicuous features in their outward appearance were the wheels, painted red, and the polished rod from the screw reversing handle on the left side of the cab to the valve gear. The weight of engine and tender totalled 82 tons in working order, but by the time the class came fully into service the permanent way of the M&SWJ had been largely relaid with the heavier (87 lb.) rails, and thus the new engines were able to display their speed to advantage, especialy on the double line between Marlborough and Weyhill.

Under GWR ownership, several of the 4−4−0s acquired taper boilers, without any great loss in the attractiveness of their appearance. They continued to work over the M&SWJ route for the rest of their days. The last to be withdrawn — in December 1928 — was No. 8 (GWR 1126).

A full list of all M&SWJ locomotives appears in the following table, which includes details of wheel diameters, cylinders, dates of building and withdrawal, and notes on subsequent histories (where appropriate).

The livery adopted for M&SWJ locomotives in the early years of this century was 'Midland red' for passenger engines and olive green for goods engines, though during World War I many were painted unlined black, and all the 0−6−0s retained this livery until grouping. The final additions to the 4−4−0 class came out in 1914 bearing the company's initials in gilt script on the tender, instead of the more conventional block lettering, and this then became the standard form on other engines.

The M&SWJ had shed accommodation at Cheltenham (14 engines), Swindon Town (6), Ludgershall (1), and Andover Junction (5). During the

A pre-grouping view of M&SWJR 0−6−0 No. 24 at Eastleigh on 17th April, 1922. Built by Beyer Peacock in 1899, this locomotive became GWR No. 1008, and was finally withdrawn in 1936. *H.C. Casserley*

M&SWJR 2−4−0 No. 11 (as GWR No. 1335) lasted until 1952; it is seen at Didcot on 16th August, 1936. *H.C. Casserley*

## Table One

### LOCOMOTIVES OF THE MIDLAND & SOUTH WESTERN JUNCTION RAILWAY

| No. | Year Built | Builders | Works No. | Type | Diameter of Coupled Wheels | | Cylinders | GWR No. | Year Withdrawn |
|---|---|---|---|---|---|---|---|---|---|
| | | | | | ft in. | in. in. | | | |
| (a) Purchased by Swindon, Marlborough & Andover Railway | | | | | | | | | |
| 1 (30) | 1881 | Dübs & Co. | 1482 | 0–6–0T | 4 0 | 15½ × 22 | | — | 1916[1] |
| 2 | 1881 | Dübs & Co. | 1483 | 0–6–0T | 4 0 | 15½ × 22 | | — | 1906[2] |
| 3 | 1881 | Dübs & Co. | 1484 | 0–6–0T | 4 0 | 15½ × 22 | | — | 1906[3] |
| 4 | 1878 | Avonside Engine Co. (for Fairlie) | — | 0–4–4T | 5 6 | 16 × 22 | | — | 1892[4] |
| 5 | 1882 | Beyer Peacock | 2230 | 2–4–0T | 5 6 | 16 × 24 | | — | 1912 |
| 6 | 1882 | Beyer Peacock | 2231 | 2–4–0T | 5 6 | 16 × 24 | | — | 1906[5] |
| 7 | 1882 | Beyer Peacock | 2232 | 2–4–0T | 5 6 | 16 × 24 | | — | 1910 |
| 8 (29) | 1884 | Beyer Peacock | 2465 | 2–4–0T | 5 6 | 17 × 24 | | — | 1918[6] |
| (b) Purchased by Midland & South Western Junction Railway | | | | | | | | | |
| 9 | 1893 | Dübs & Co. | 3076 | 4–4–0 | 6 0 | 17 × 24 | | 1127 | 1924 |
| 10 | 1894 | Dübs & Co. | 3165 | 2–4–0 | 5 6 | 17 × 24 | | 1334 | 1952 |
| 11 | 1894 | Dübs & Co. | 3166 | 2–4–0 | 5 6 | 17 × 24 | | 1335 | 1952 [7] |
| 12 | 1894 | Dübs & Co. | 3167 | 2–4–0 | 5 6 | 17 × 24 | | 1336 | 1954 |
| 13 | 1894 | Dübs & Co. | 3168 | 0–6–0T | 4 7 | 17 × 24 | | 825 | 1926 |
| 4 (14) | 1894 | Dübs & Co. | 3164 | 0–6–0T | 4 7 | 17 × 24 | | 843 | 1926 |
| 14 | 1895 | Beyer Peacock | 3679 | 2–6–0 | 4 0 | 18 × 26 | | — | 1914[8] |
| 15 | 1895 | Beyer Peacock | 3682 | 0–4–4T | 5 2 | 17 × 24 | | 23 | 1930[9] |
| 16 | 1897 | Beyer Peacock | 3884 | 2–6–0 | 4 0 | 18 × 26 | | 24 | 1930[10] |
| 17 | 1897 | Sharp Stewart | 4300 | 4–4–4T | 5 3 | 17 × 24 | | 25 | 1927 |
| 18 | 1897 | Sharp Stewart | 4301 | 4–4–4T | 5 3 | 17 × 24 | | 27* | 1929[11] |
| 19 | 1899 | Beyer Peacock | 4097 | 0–6–0 | 5 2½ | 18 × 26 | | 1003* | 1936 |
| 20 | 1899 | Beyer Peacock | 4098 | 0–6–0 | 5 2½ | 18 × 26 | | 1004* | 1934 |
| 21 | 1899 | Beyer Peacock | 4099 | 0–6–0 | 5 2½ | 18 × 26 | | 1005* | 1938 |
| 22 | 1899 | Beyer Peacock | 4100 | 0–6–0 | 5 2½ | 18 × 26 | | 1006* | 1934 |
| 23 | 1899 | Beyer Peacock | 4101 | 0–6–0 | 5 2½ | 18 × 26 | | 1007* | 1937 |
| 24 | 1899 | Beyer Peacock | 4102 | 0–6–0 | 5 2½ | 18 × 26 | | 1008* | 1936 |
| 25 | 1902 | Beyer Peacock | 4440 | 0–6–0 | 5 2½ | 18 × 26 | | 1009* | 1935 |
| 26 | 1902 | Beyer Peacock | 4441 | 0–6–0 | 5 2½ | 18 × 26 | | 1010* | 1934 |
| 27 | 1902 | Beyer Peacock | 4442 | 0–6–0 | 5 2½ | 18 × 26 | | 1011* | 1937 |
| 28 | 1902 | Beyer Peacock | 4443 | 0–6–0 | 5 2½ | 18 × 26 | | 1013* | 1937 |
| 1 | 1905 | North British Loco Co. Ltd | 16817 | 4–4–0 | 5 9 | 18 × 26 | | 1119 | 1935 |
| 2 | 1909 | North British Loco Co. Ltd | 18791 | 4–4–0 | 5 9 | 18 × 26 | | 1120* | 1931 |
| 3 | 1909 | North British Loco Co. Ltd | 18792 | 4–4–0 | 5 9 | 18 × 26 | | 1121* | 1936 |
| 4 | 1914 | North British Loco Co. Ltd | 20539 | 4–4–0 | 5 9 | 18 × 26 | | 1122 | 1935 |
| 5 | 1912 | North British Loco Co. Ltd | 19755 | 4–4–0 | 5 9 | 18 × 26 | | 1123* | 1938 |
| 6 | 1910 | North British Loco Co. Ltd | 19133 | 4–4–0 | 5 9 | 18 × 26 | | 1124* | 1935 |
| 7 | 1911 | North British Loco Co. Ltd | 19314 | 4–4–0 | 5 9 | 18 × 26 | | 1125 | 1932 |
| 8 | 1912 | North British Loco Co. Ltd | 19756 | 4–4–0 | 5 9 | 18 × 26 | | 1126* | 1938 |
| 31 | 1914 | North British Loco Co. Ltd | 20540 | 4–4–0 | 5 9 | 18 × 26 | | 1128* | 1935 |

1 Sold to Bute Works Supply Co.
2 Sold to S. Pearson & Son.
3 Sold to S. Pearson & Son.
4 Purchased by SM&A in 1882.
5 Sold to Isle of Wight Central Railway (IWCR No. 7, S. Railway No. W7, scrapped 1926).
6 Sold to Wake, Darlington.
7 Fitted with GW Belpaire boilers in 1924 and transferred to Reading district.
8 Frame and wheels sold to Wake, Darlington in 1918.
9 Rebuilt with GW S/11 boiler, 1925.
10 Fitted with Belpaire boiler 1925. Transferred to Bristol area.
11 Transferred to Kidderminster area after re-boilering in 1925.

* Rebuilt with GWR standard taper boilers.

(Figures in brackets indicate engine numbers at date of withdrawal.)

early period when the company owned relatively few engines their care and maintenance were the responsibility of a locomotive foreman, who worked under the supervision of the Engineer or General Manager. In 1903 the post was raised to the status of locomotive and carriage superintendent and was filled from then until 1923 by James Tyrell, who went originally to the company as a driver in 1890.

### Passenger and Freight Stock

In the days of greatest poverty, the stock of vehicles in Midland & South Western Junction service was not only scanty in amount, but was also precariously held against attempts at seizure by unsatisfied creditors. The passenger vehicles comprised an assortment of 24 four- and six-wheeled coaches acquired, with other stock, from the Metropolitan Railway Carriage & Wagon Co. under a 'hire-purchase' arrangement in 1881 and 1882. The debt on the vehicles mounted up, and the carriage company tried on several occasions to regain possession but were successfully staved off. The coaches, which were painted cream above waist level and brown below, became very much the worse for wear; the M&SWJ could not afford to repaint them, and moreover it was urged that 'any outlay for that purpose would be almost useless without a carriage shed to protect the vehicles from the weather'.

In 1891 the M&SWJ gave an undertaking to the Board of Trade to fit its coaches with continuous automatic vacuum brakes, and for this purpose the company had to borrow money from the L&SWR. Stock was frequently hired or borrowed from the L&SWR. Some additions purchased in 1896 were charged up in the capital account of the Marlborough & Grafton Railway and for a short time were technically its property.

However, proper replacements, when they came, were very good, and the M&SWJ at length possessed a stock of vehicles of which any small railway company could have been proud. The standard passenger coaches were non-corridor four-wheel bogie vehicles, steam-heated and lit by electricity. They were painted 'Midland red' to match the passenger engines and rode very well; some of them were purchased second-hand from the Midland Railway in 1910–12 at an average price of £165 per coach.

Information on Midland & South Western Junction Railway freight stock is sparse in relation to the wealth of information published about its locomotives, and one wishes that the pioneer railway photographers had taken just a few broadside photographs of M&SWJ wagons in everyday service. As a general rule, however, it can be said that the railway's small fleet of goods vehicles included the usual open wagons and covered vans, together with a number of specialised vehicles for the carriage of horses, timber or machinery. Midland & South Western Junction freight stock was painted dark grey and carried the company's initials in white letters shaded in black.

One of the MSWJ 4−4−4Ts glides round the curves near Marlborough station with a
four coach southbound local train. Note the driver about to hand over the token to the
signalman.                                                            L.C.G.B. Collection.

An unidentified MSWJ 0−6−0 stands beneath the footbridge serving the island platform at Swindon, in the early 1900s.                                   L.C.G.B. Collection

Typical MSWJ rolling stock; brake van No. 10 (*above*) and unfitted goods van No. 158 (*below*) seen as new when built by the Gloucester Carriage and Wagon Co.

*H.M.R.S. Collection*

Two of the MSWJ open wagons; note that on Midland & South Western Junction freight vehicles the 'MSWJR' lettering was shaded (black or sometimes very dark blue); photographed new in September 1896. *H.M.R.S. Collection*

A MSWJ six-wheeled passenger third vehicle No. 20 in its original brown and cream livery. Built by the Gloucester Carriage & Wagon Company in 1896.

*H.M.R.S. Collection*

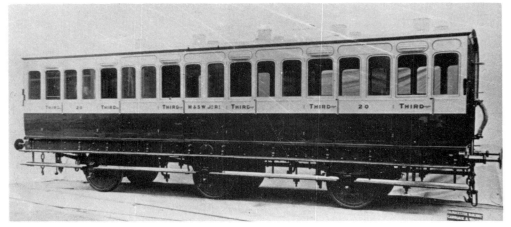

One of the two Beyer Peacock 'Colonial style', 2−6−0s passes the Marlborough, Great Western station, with a southbound freight working.           *L.C.G.B. Collection*

A Midland and South Western Junction 4−4−0 seen here departing from Andover Junction with a MSWJ working.           *L.C.G.B. Collection*

Front of Manoeuvres Folder, 1913.

*T.B. Sands Collection*

A general view of Cheltenham Lansdown station, the northern terminus for most of the MSWJ services.
*H.C. Casserley*

Cheltenham Leckhampton GWR station, looking towards Cheltenham on the 29th August, 1959.
*Lens of Sutton*

The diminutive station of Charlton Kings facing Cheltenham as photographed on 1st May, 1956.                                                                 *H.C. Casserley*

A general view of the MSWJ station at Andoversford & Dowdeswell before the singling of the lines; this station lost its passenger services after the grouping.
*Mowat Collection*

Withington was situated on the double track section from Andoversford; it had austere brick buildings, of similar design to those at Foss Cross (both stations were opened in 1891). The line was singled in 1928.                   *H.C. Casserley*

Withington station, looking north towards Andoversford in the 1930s after the singling of the line.                                            *Mowat Collection*

# Chapter Four

## The Route Described

The Midland & South Western Junction Railway's foothold in Cheltenham was both firm and extensive. It leased in perpetuity the land for its goods accommodation at High Street, had its own engine shed and turntable, and maintained certain sidings jointly with the Midland. It had also the full run of the Midland passenger station at Lansdown, at a rent of £500 per annum, plus a share of the working expenses calculated in proportion to the number of passengers booked by each company annually. Moreover, M&SWJ trains were able to use the through platforms, and were not strictly confined to the bay on the east side which was their normal preserve.

Train loadings were governed by the climb out of Cheltenham, which included 3½ miles at 1 in 62 on the Great Western line from Charlton Kings to Andoversford Junction. On the M&SWJ proper the ruling gradient was 1 in 75; the longest unbroken stretch was of 1¾ miles from Rushey Platt to Swindon Town.

### Into the Cotswolds

The junction at Andoversford was placed east of the Great Western station in accordance with a deviation authorised in 1884 in substitution for a junction farther west which would have enabled M&SWJ trains to by-pass the station on a much easier curve, the course of which survives as a length of old embankment. This abandoned earthwork has sometimes been taken to mark the beginning of one of the abortive extensions of 1898 or 1899, though in fact these were never authorised, let alone started, and the plans show that they would have taken a route well removed from that of the abandoned embankment.*

No M&SWJ trains called at the GWR station before 1st October, 1904, and very few thereafter until grouping, when the separate Midland & South Western station (Andoversford & Dowdeswell) became redundant and was closed on 1st April, 1927. It lay ½ mile south of the junction and was called Dowdeswell until 1st October, 1892.

Having reached their own line beyond Andoversford, trains headed southwards through picturesque Cotswold countryside, and soon reached the first intermediate station at Withington. A two platform stopping place, Withington was similar to its counterparts elsewhere on the line, with simple, brick station buildings on the up (i.e. northbound) platform.

### Chedworth

The climb into the Cotswolds was resumed at Withington, continuing with gradients of 1 in 75 through Chedworth woods and tunnel to a summit 637 ft above sea level south of Chedworth station. The latter had no facilities for public goods traffic, which was handled at Foss Cross only a mile farther on, but at the close of World War I a government siding, called Chedworth Wood siding, was put in under the auspices of the wartime Timber Control Department.

---

* In 1865 the East Gloucestershire Railway started building its own (abortive) line at Andoversford and some of the abandoned earthworks at this point are of EGR, not MSWJ origin.

A general view of the passenger-only station at Chedworth, facing Cheltenham on 2nd October, 1960.                                                                    *R.M. Casserley*

Chedworth in the early 1930s, shortly after the line between Andoversford and Cirencester was singled. The main station building (*left*) was the second to occupy the site, the original one being little more than a waiting shelter.              *Mowat Collection*

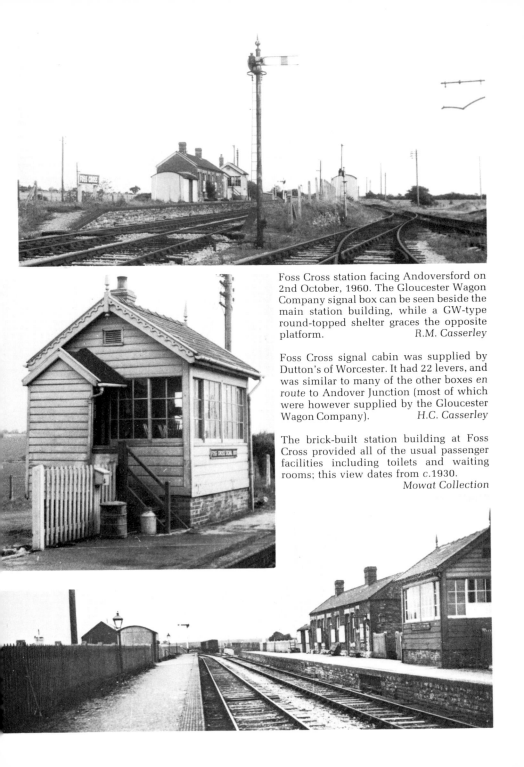

Foss Cross station facing Andoversford on 2nd October, 1960. The Gloucester Wagon Company signal box can be seen beside the main station building, while a GW-type round-topped shelter graces the opposite platform. *R.M. Casserley*

Foss Cross signal cabin was supplied by Dutton's of Worcester. It had 22 levers, and was similar to many of the other boxes *en route* to Andover Junction (most of which were however supplied by the Gloucester Wagon Company). *H.C. Casserley*

The brick-built station building at Foss Cross provided all of the usual passenger facilities including toilets and waiting rooms; this view dates from *c.*1930. *Mowat Collection*

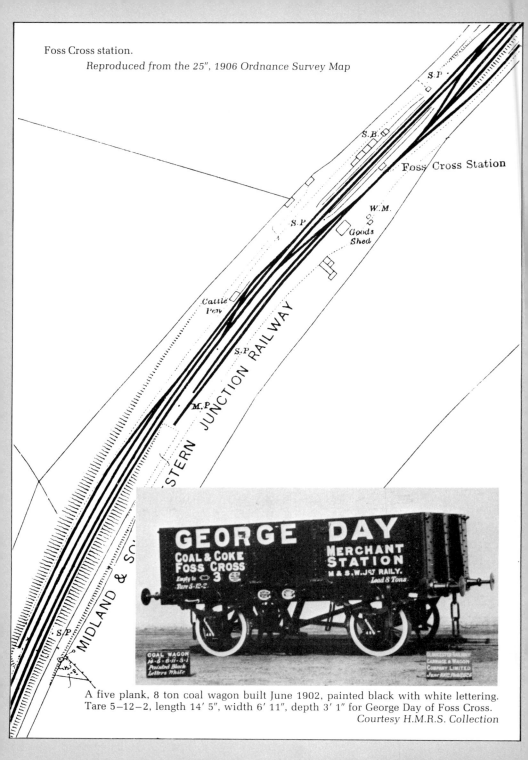

Foss Cross station.

*Reproduced from the 25", 1906 Ordnance Survey Map*

A five plank, 8 ton coal wagon built June 1902, painted black with white lettering.
Tare 5–12–2, length 14' 5", width 6' 11", depth 3' 1" for George Day of Foss Cross.
*Courtesy H.M.R.S. Collection*

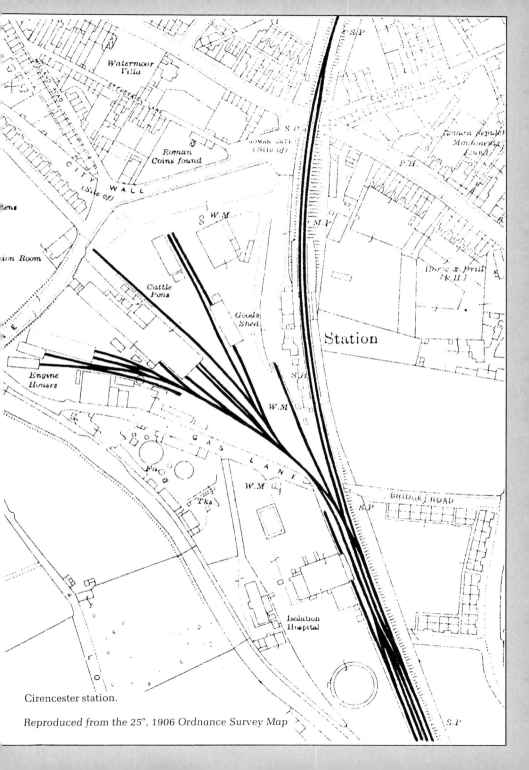

Cirencester station.

Reproduced from the 25″, 1906 Ordnance Survey Map

An early view of Cirencester MSWJ station, showing the original (pre-1912) water tank and the corrugated iron building that functioned as engineering department offices.

*Loco. Publishing Co. Collection  H.B. Priestley*

Cirencester MSWJ station, looking north towards Andoversford on 10th March, 1956. The standard Midland & South Western Junction Railway signal box (*left*) was a typical Gloucester Wagon Company product; the water tower visible beyond originally had a much smaller tank. *R.M. Casserley*

Cirencester station, looking south on 8th June, 1934. The factory visible beyond the platform was Cirencester gas works – a useful source of traffic for the MSWJ line.
*Mowat Collection*

The M&SWJ works at Cirencester was closed in 1925, and the site was later used as a scrap yard. This 1956 view shows the ruins of the locomotive shops, which were once served by two sidings which entered the stylish elliptical doorway. The extension seen to the left of the main block was dated '1915'. *H.C. Casserley*

Cirencester looking north on 8th June, 1934 and showing the goods shed (*left*) position relative to the station. *Mowat Collection*

South Cerney, looking north in June 1934. The original signal cabin shown here was abolished in 1942 when the GWR-type box shown below was brought into use.

*Mowat Collection*

South Cerney facing Swindon on 24th April, 1958. The main station building was on the northbound or up platform, the only passenger accommodation on the down side being a simple waiting shelter. Note the multiple-arched road overbridge.

*R.M. Casserley*

Class 4, 2−6−0 No. 76065 coasts past the standard Great Western style signal cabin at
South Cerney station on the 29th April, 1958.                    *H.C. Casserley*

A view of Cricklade station looking south, showing the lines running to the cattle pens
and goods shed (*left*). Photographed in 1934.                    *Mowat Collection*

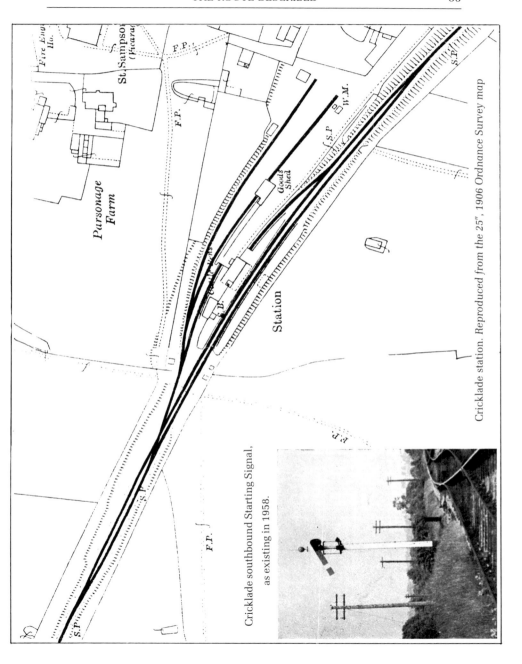

Cricklade southbound Starting Signal,
as existing in 1958.

Cricklade station. Reproduced from the 25", 1906 Ordnance Survey map

Cricklade signal box was another Gloucester Wagon Company design with 14 levers; the tiny window situated high in the end gables was a typical GWCo. feature, although the curious projecting window seen to the right was a later addition. When first erected the box was built entirely of timber, but it was subsequently rebuilt with a brick tower storey, as shown in this *c.*1950s view. *Oakwood Collection*

Cricklade station, looking north around 1960. The passing loop at Cricklade was (1923) over 300 yds long and could accommodate 18-coach trains. The M&SWJ-type gabled station building measured approximately 66 ft × 24 ft, and the nearby goods sidings could hold around 80 wagons. *Oakwood Collection*

When first opened Chedworth had been a tiny, single platform station, but a second platform and new station buildings were added when the line between Withington and Foss Cross was doubled in June 1902. The station buildings were of wooden construction, and a small canopy was provided for the benefit of waiting travellers.

## Foss Cross

Still heading southwards, trains continued along the line to Foss Cross (15 miles 43 chains) — a somewhat remote station lying in open, often windswept countryside. The main buildings, of brick construction, were on the up platform, and there was a simple round-topped waiting shelter on the opposite side. A gabled signal cabin stood beside the station buildings on the up platform; like most other Midland & South Western Junction cabins, this wooden box had been supplied by a specialist signalling contractor — in this case Dutton's of Worcester.

The descent from Foss Cross included two miles of 1 in 80 falling gradients, ending in a sharp and unexpected turn to the west along the line of the abortive branch to Fairford.

## Cirencester

Maintaining its westerly heading, the railway entered the important intermediate station at Cirencester. Two platforms were provided, the main station building being on the up side; the use of Cotswold stone added a note of distinction to this otherwise simple building, and a full length canopy protected the platform frontage. Other structures on the up platform included the usual Gloucester Wagon Company-type signal cabin and a substantial stone-built water tower.

Cirencester rivalled Swindon as the administrative centre of the M&SWJ. It was from there that Sam Fay directed the affairs of the company, and there also were established in 1895 the engine repair shops, on a site immediately west of the station.

From Cirencester the Midland & South Western Junction line turned south-eastwards, and with the Thames & Severn Canal running parallel to the left, trains entered what might be called the 'milk belt' of the M&SWJ — the lush dairy farming country of the Vale of the White Horse, with Cricklade, across the boundary in Wiltshire, as its centre.

## South Cerney

Lengthy stops for the loading or unloading of milk churns were often the rule at wayside stations such as South Cerney, which contributed little else in the way of originating traffic. South Cerney was a passing place with up and down platforms and a multiple-arched road overbridge to the south. There was a hip-roofed station building on the up platform and a tiny waiting shelter on the down side. The modest track layout was originally controlled from a small Gloucester Wagon Company-type signal cabin at the

The tiny station at Blunsdon, seen in 1934 looking northwards from the adjacent road overbridge. The curious wooden structure seen in the foreground is probably the remnants of a covered milk loading stage.                    *Mowat Collection*

Blunsdon station.                    *Reproduced from the 1911, 25" Ordnance Survey map*

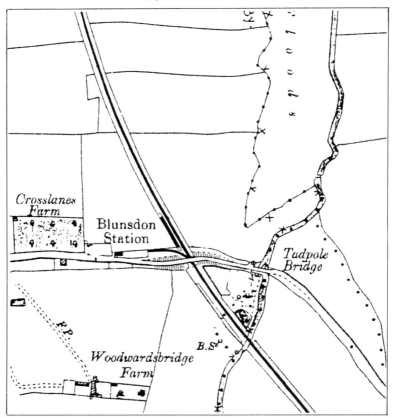

north end of the down platform, but a standard Great Western gabled box was later erected here.

At the time of its opening the station had been called Cerney & Ashton Keynes, but its name was later shortened to become simply Cerney; later still, in July 1924, the station was renamed South Cerney.

## Cricklade

Leaving South Cerney, trains continued south-east towards the Gloucestershire–Wiltshire border. Although the countryside visible on either side of the line was surprisingly flat, nearby villages such as Cerney Wick and Down Ampney contained many attractive Cotswold buildings. Down Ampney was also of interest in that it was the birthplace of Ralph Vaughan Williams (1872–1958), the great composer whose many works epitomise the English countryside at its best.

Crossing the River Thames — little more than a winding stream at this point — the single line entered Wiltshire and approached the Thameside town of Cricklade. The station here was another typical Midland & South Western Junction stopping place, with a crossing loop, up and down platforms, and a three-siding goods yard on the down side. The station building, with its projecting canopy, was similar to that at Cirencester, albeit of brick rather than Cotswold stone construction. Other facilities at Cricklade included the usual Gloucester Wagon Company-style signal cabin, a small waiting shelter on the up platform, and an additional dead-end loading bay at the south end of the down platform with accommodation for just 8 wagons.

From Cricklade, the line turned southwards, and down trains soon reached Blunsdon. One of the smaller intermediate stations, Blunsdon had just one platform and a single siding; it was served by very few passenger trains, the last service to call being a solitary Sunday working which finally ceased stopping in the Autumn of 1924.

## Swindon

Milk was the staple traffic at Moredon Platform (opened on 25th March, 1913) and latterly at Rushey Platt, which was closed to passengers on 1st October, 1905. Rushey Platt station, when first opened on 13th December, 1883, had four platforms, two on the curve to the GWR and two at a higher level on the line to Cirencester; these platforms were linked by a subway, which was blocked up in 1907. The station building (still standing in 1958) was on the southbound platform on the curve, from which, as already mentioned, passenger trains were withdrawn in 1885. The curve remained open for the exchange of goods, which under the original agreement, was effected at Swindon Transfer, east of the GWR station, the M&SWJ being responsible for working the transfer trips. In July 1891, the M&SWJ gave notice to terminate this arrangement, and from the end of that year traffic was exchanged at Rushey Platt Junction, each company working to that point with its own engines. This continued until 18th January, 1922, when

A glimpse in 1934 of the rarely-photographed milk platform at Moredon; the platform was only 40 ft long, and few trains called here.                    *Mowat Collection*

Local private owner wagon for J. Manning & Sons of Cricklade built by the Gloucester Carriage Wagon Co.

the GWR began to work freight trips through to Swindon Town.

The M&SWJ station at Swindon (situated off Newport Street in the old town, close to the cattle market) was well placed so long as this remained the heart of the town's commercial life; but in course of time there came a steady drift of shops and offices to the new town centre at the bottom of the hill.

In acreage and extent of platform accommodation Swindon Town was surpassed by Ludgershall, but in other respects it was the outstanding station on the M&SWJ — spacious and well laid out, with the main buildings, including a refreshment room, on the southbound (down) platform. The company's head offices occupied an adjacent house, called The Croft, in which they were established when the line was opened in 1881. Before that date the official address was 42 Cricklade Street, Swindon, where the solicitor, J. C. Townsend, had his office.

The station itself was enlarged in 1904–5 by creating an island platform on the up side to give two up platform roads, beyond which a further through road gave access to a 55 ft diameter turntable at the north end. Double line block was worked between the 'A' and 'B' signal boxes north and south of the station.

### Chiseldon

The high barrier of the Marlborough Down confronted the railway south of Swindon, offering at first sight few obvious sources of revenue; for across that delightful but thinly populated tract of open country it was possible, not so many years ago, to walk all day and meet scarcely a soul.

Entering the immense, empty landscapes of the Downs, M&SWJ trains ran south-eastwards to Chiseldon, a two platform station, situated some 3 miles 11 chains beyond Swindon Town. Built on a gentle curve, Chiseldon had a small, hip-roofed station building on the down side and a simple waiting shelter on the opposite platform. There was a small goods yard on the down side and a road overbridge spanned the line at the southern end of the platforms; the original M&SWJ signal box was later superseded by a standard Great Western cabin.

A hidden asset at Chiseldon and neighbouring stations was racehorse traffic from the area's famous training stables, while in later years there was added military traffic from the barracks at Chiseldon, for which a siding connection was opened in September 1914. But the horse-boxes predominated, and their attachment or detachment at Chiseldon, Ogbourne, and Marlborough was a time-wasting operation second only to the handling of milk churns between Cirencester and Swindon.

Departing from Chiseldon trains crossed the historic Ridgeway, and turning southwards, reached Chiseldon Camp Halt. Opened on 1st December, 1930, this sleeper-built stopping place was situated on the up side of the line. A simple, open-fronted shelter was provided for the convenience of waiting travellers, and at night the halt was illuminated by two electric lights bolted to creosoted wooden posts.

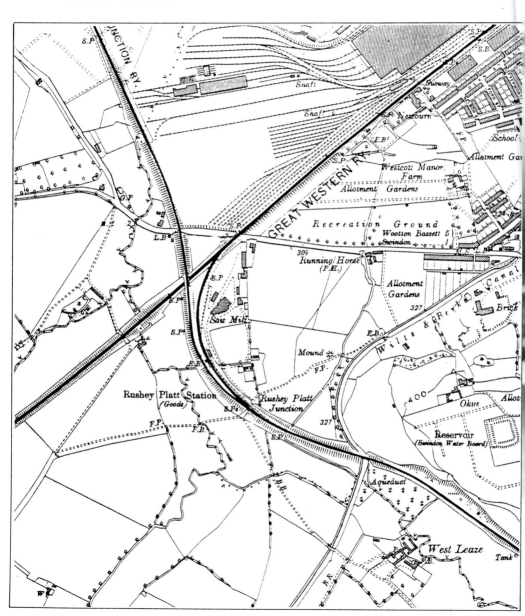

Lines in the Rushey Platt area around 1925; the MSWJ route runs from north to south while the GWR main line extends from the SW to the NE. Part of the Great Western Locomotive Works can be seen to the north of the main line. (This 6 inch OS Map does not differentiate between single and multiple track, but the junction layout is clearly shown.) *Reproduced from the 6″, 1906 Ordnance Survey map*

Rushey Platt station, looking north towards the GWR main line in 1932 (compare with map on previous page). The high level platforms were (in later years at least) merely short staff platforms. *Mowat Collection*

An interesting glimpse inside Rushey Platt signal cabin; this box had 30 levers, though in this 1932 view several appear to be white-painted 'spares'. *Mowat Collection*

The low level platform at Rushey Platt, showing the standard MSWJ station building; photographed in 1932, this station was closed to passenger traffic as far back as 1905! *Mowat Collection*

Swindon Town station.     Reproduced from the  6″, 1906 Ordnance Survey map

A panoramic view of Swindon Town, looking north towards Cheltenham. The Midland & South Western Junction Railway's offices can be seen to the right, and the 55 ft diameter turntable is prominent to the left of the picture.     *Oakwood Collection*

A view south from the down platform at Swindon Town, showing the large goods shed (*left*) and an assortment of PW huts and lamp rooms (*centre*). The goods shed was 150 ft long, and contained an internal loading platform.     *Oakwood Collection*

View north from the down platform at Swindon Town, with the island platform visible to the left; both platforms were over 500 ft long. The main station building (right) was similar to its counterpart elsewhere on the M&SWJ system, albeit with a 2-storey portion at the southern end.

*Oakwood Collection*

Chiseldon station looking north towards Swindon and Cheltenham. The standard GWR signal box seen in the distance was built in 1942 as a replacement for an earlier M&SWJ box. Note the way in which the saw-toothed platform canopy has been cut back to accommodate modern rolling stock (this was probably carried out during World War II when the M&SWJ carried much extra traffic).    *Douglas Thompson*

A useful view of Chiseldon, looking south in the direction of Southampton. The structure on the extreme right was used as a goods store, while the brick-built shed between the signal cabin and the station building was a parcels office – both were added during the GWR era.    *H.B. Priestley*

Opened on 1st December, 1930, Chiseldon Camp Halt was situated at 41 miles from Cheltenham; its open-fronted waiting shelter was not of GWR design, and some M&SWJ components may well have been used in its construction. This March 1958 view is facing north towards Marlborough.                    *R.M. Casserley*

'55XX' class 2−6−2T No. 5509 stands on the down line at Ogbourne with a pick-up freight working. The date is 12th June, 1959.                    *H.B. Priestley*

Ogbourne stables platform was served by a loop line. This was located at Ogbourne St Andrew just south of Ogbourne St George station.   *Courtesy Railway Magazine*

Ogbourne station.   *Reproduced from the 25″, 1906 Ordnance Survey map*

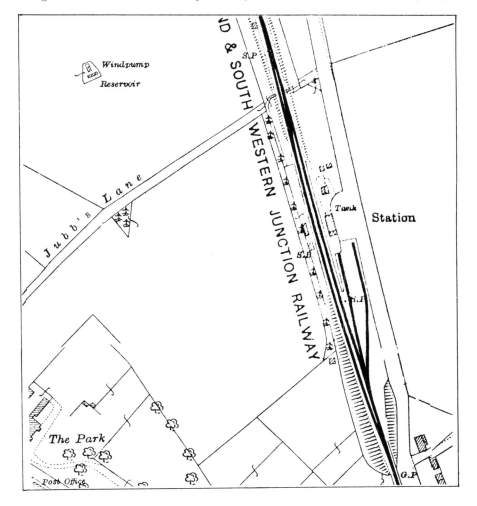

View south from Ogbourne's down platform after closure; the passing loop here was signalled for 2-way working (after 1952). *Oakwood Collection*

Ogbourne station, looking north towards Andoversford in the 1930s. The MSWJ signal box was replaced in 1943, but the old box was not demolished until the 1950s.
*Douglas Thompson*

## Ogbourne

Continuing due south, the railway made its way into the chalk downs through a geological feature known as the Ogbourne wind-gap, and with great, rolling hills now visible on both sides of the line, southbound trains reached Ogbourne (43 miles 27 chains).

Another two platform station, Ogbourne's track layout incorporated a crossing loop, with a goods yard on the down side containing two dead-end sidings. The station building was situated on the down platform, and there was a waiting shelter and signal cabin on the up side of the line; a new, GWR-type box was subsequently erected on a fresh site at the north end of the down platform.

Falling steadily, the route then continued towards Marlborough, which was approached by a remarkable horse-shoe curve, followed by a final climb at 1 in 75 to the platform end.

## Marlborough

Although only two platforms were needed Marlborough was, as far as the M&SWJ was concerned, a place of some significance, and its relative import- ance was underlined by the provision of larger-than-usual station buildings on the up platform. The main block was a hip-roofed structure with a projecting canopy, but there was, in addition, a gabled-ended extension on the south side. Facilities on the down platform consisted of a waiting shelter and signal box, while the nearby goods yard — on the up side — was equipped with a large goods shed.

In Midland & South Western Junction days the station had possessed a highly-polished brass handbell which was kept in the signal box (then at the Swindon end of the southbound platform) and rung with vigour and effect on the approach of a passenger train booked to stop, to spur the flagging steps of passengers trudging up the hill from the town. It bore the initials of the Swindon Marlborough & Andover Railway, but unfortunately the letter 'M' had been cast upside down! Then there was the convivial atmosphere of the refreshment room, which, complete with annexe and dart board for regulars, had long served as the 'local' for that end of the town.

Before entering Marlborough tunnel (approached from the north by a curve of 20 chains radius) the railway passed that former scene of frustration and delay, 'Marlborough South Junction'. The connection with the Great Western was removed after the opening of the Marlborough & Grafton line in 1898, but it was restored for wagon transfers after grouping and was brought back into use on 23rd November, 1926.

On the high plateau south of Marlborough tunnel, the M&SWJ again reached a summit over 600 feet above sea level and then descended at 1 in 100 through the fringes of Savernake Forest, within sight of the GWR branch for two or three miles — a circumstance which sometimes gave rise to impromptu and spirited races between trains on the rival systems!

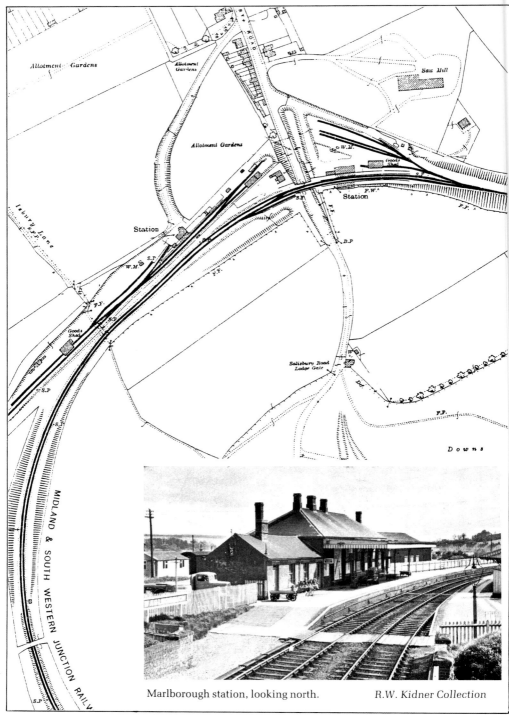

Marlborough station, looking north.  R.W. Kidner Collection

Marlborough station.  *Reproduced from the 25″, 1906 Ordnance Survey Map*

An unidentified MSWJ 4–4–0 stands in the down platform at Marlborough in the years before World War I; the austere water tower was dismantled around 1917.

*Ken Nunn Collection*

A 'Duke' 4−4−0 at Marlborough Low Level on 15th July, 1933.     *R.W. Kidner*

Marlborough's down platform was equipped with a relatively large waiting shelter built mainly of corrugated iron; the crossing loop here was signalled for conventional up/down working, although the double track section beyond was latterly worked as two single lines.     *Oakwood Collection*

Small-wheeled '55XX' class 2−6−2T No. 5510 enters Marlborough M&SWJ station with a local passenger train on 1st September, 1952. *H.C. Casserley*

Another view of Marlborough Low Level, looking south towards Andover Junction. When first built, the station had four very tall chimneys, but these were later cut down leaving the somewhat stubby examples seen here. *Oakwood Collection*

In 1933 the GWR brought a new signal box into use in connection with its remodelling of the lines between Marlborough and Wolfhall Junction; at the same time Marlborough GWR station (part of which can be seen to the right) was closed to passenger traffic. Photograph taken 7th July, 1933. *Mowat Collection*

The former Marlborough Railway terminus remained in being as a goods station, while all passenger traffic was concentrated in the MSWJ Low Level station (seen on the extreme right). *Douglas Thompson*

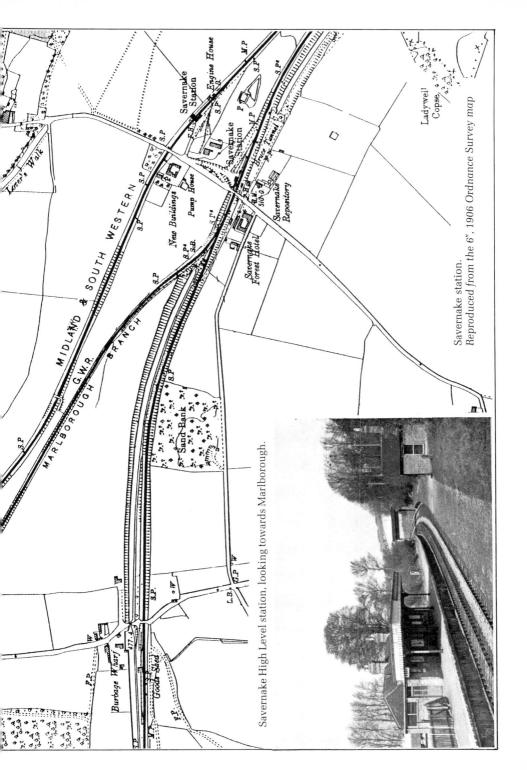

Savernake High Level station, looking towards Marlborough.

Savernake station.
Reproduced from the 6", 1906 Ordnance Survey map

A rear view of Savernake High Level station in 1959; the Marquess of Ailesbury's private waiting room can be glimpsed in the left background, while the Gloucester Wagon Co. signal box is visible to the right. *H.C. Casserley*

Savernake High Level station, seen from a passing train on 1st September, 1952; this former M&SWJ station was reduced in status in 1933 (when its passing loop was taken out of use for passenger traffic) and the station was finally closed in 1958, when services were diverted into the nearby Low Level station. *H.C. Casserley*

No. 6372 2−6−0 passing Grafton South Junction with the R.C.T.S. Wessex Wyvern special *en route* from Weymouth to Andover, 8th July, 1956.　　　　　*L. Elsie*

An early 1928 view of Grafton South Junction.　　　　　*Mowat Collection*

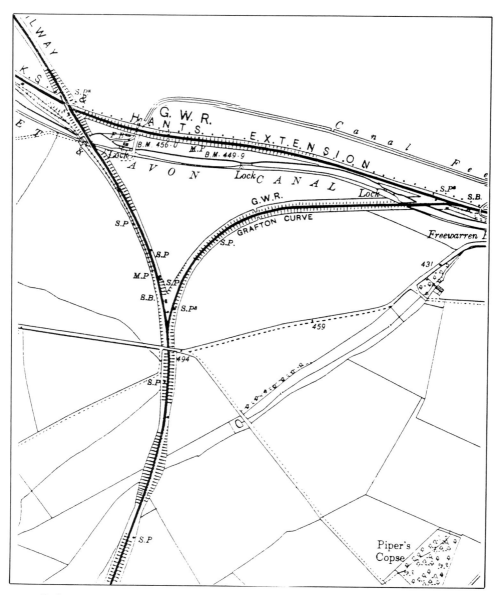

Grafton Junction.    *Reproduced from the 6″, 1906 Ordnance Survey map*

## Savernake

Savernake (Midland & South Western Junction) station, 200 yds north of the GWR station, boasted a footbridge (found nowhere else on the line except at Swindon and Ludgershall), a private waiting room for the Marquess of Ailesbury, and in spring and summer a floral display of outstanding beauty.

At Wolfhall, beyond Savernake, two connections from the Great Western came into the M&SWJ facing south — a single line spur from the west, and a double line curve from the east. The single line spur was formed from the tag end of the original southern section of the M&SWJ, which had been left as a disused siding on the opening of the Marlborough & Grafton line, running south from the junction with the GWR to a dead end and trailing connection with the M&SWJ. This connection and a loop siding were used for wagon transfers from 1st November, 1900 and later the former was replaced by a facing connection, controlled from a new signal box named Wolfhall Junction (M&SWJ), opened on 28th July, 1902, when a second loop siding was added.

The double line loop from the east, called the Grafton curve, was owned by the GWR and was built under an agreement of 1903, whereby the GWR secured running powers over the M&SWJ from Wolfhall Junction to Ludgershall. As part of this development, Wolfhall Junction (M&SWJ) box was moved from its earlier (1902) site to a more convenient spot farther south, where it could control the junctions with both the east and west connecting spurs; the new and much enlarged box was opened on 20th August, 1905. Grafton curve was completed on 6th September, 1905 and was used largely for military traffic of an intermittent nature and also, after grouping, by occasional excursion trains; it was closed on 5th May, 1957.

## Grafton & Burbage

Grafton & Burbage station (55 miles 22 chains) was only a short distance further on. Situated just 1 mile 70 chains from Savernake, the station had up and down platforms, the up, or northbound platform being slightly shorter than its counterpart on the down side of the line. A lengthy goods siding diverged from the up main line at the south of the up platform and curved around the passenger station before rejoining the running line at the northern end of the station. Three short spurs branched out from this main siding, and there was an additional dead-end siding on the down side.

In architectural terms, Grafton & Burbage was similar to most of the other Midland & South Western Junction stations, in that its main building was a simple, brick-built structure with a hipped roof and a projecting canopy. There was a standard Gloucester Wagon Company signal box at the southern end of the down platform while, on the up side, a tiny platform shelter provided scant comfort for the occasional traveller.

On a footnote, it is interesting to recall that Grafton station was, for a few years, the starting point of a standard gauge mineral line running eastward for about two miles to some brickworks at Dodsdown, near Bedwyn. The

Grafton & Burbage, looking north on 15th March, 1958. The Gloucester Wagon Company signal box was unusual in that it lacked floor level windows. *H.C. Casserley*

Grafton station facing Andover on 15th March, 1958. Note the Southern Region signals; the goods line seen diverging to the right was not signalled for through running, and there was no facing connection in the up direction. *R.M. Casserley*

mineral rights at Dodsdown were leased by the Marquess of Ailesbury in 1902 to A. J. Keeble, of Peterborough, who built the line from Grafton and worked it, apparently with two steam locomotives, on payment of £50 per annum to the Marquess for wayleaves. It was closed and dismantled in 1910, though its course can still be traced in many places.

## Collingbourne

From Grafton the line dropped towards Salisbury Plain, and with the Marlborough to Andover road running parallel to the right, trains reached Collingbourne Kingston. There was no station here in M&SWJ days, but this deficiency was rectified by the opening of Collingbourne Kingston Halt on 1st April, 1932.

The route then continued to Collingbourne Ducis, which was a little over one mile from Collingbourne Kingston, and connected to it by the contiguous hamlet of Collingbourne Sutton. Collingbourne station (59 miles 42 chains) was situated on the western side of the village, and the main buildings were, for this reason, sited on the up platform (Victorian stations were usually arranged with their ticket offices and waiting rooms on the most convenient side of the line in relation to the towns or villages that they purported to serve). A hip-roofed station building was again provided, together with the usual waiting shelter on the opposite platform.

## Ludgershall

The southernmost stretch of the Midland & South Western Junction Railway — the section that bordered Salisbury Plain — had about it a distinct military atmosphere, overwhelming in wartime and never wholly absent. It centred round Ludgershall, where the original station building was quite dwarfed by the lavish expanse of platform accommodation, added between 1900 and 1902 when Ludgershall became the junction for Tidworth and an important military railhead in its own right. At that time many extra sidings were provided in the angle between the main line and branch, together with a turntable and a small engine shed.

On the Tidworth branch the gradients were 1 in 95 rising for a mile from Perham box, with a corresponding descent at 1 in 90 into Tidworth, where the station lay astride the county boundary. It was said that, when buying a ticket, the passenger was in Hampshire and the booking clerk in Wiltshire!

## Weyhill

The final 7½ miles of line between Ludgershall and Andover Junction, most of which were in Hampshire, provided a fine galloping ground for southbound trains — thanks to a combination of falling gradients and a relatively straight alignment. In M&SWJ days some southbound non-stop workings were booked to cover this stretch in only ten minutes, inclusive of a slowing at Weyhill to pick up the single line tablet.

Weyhill (64 miles 74 chains), the penultimate stopping place, exhibited

Collingbourne, looking north towards Swindon and Andoversford on 12th August, 1959. The hip-roofed station building was a typical MSWJ structure; the platforms were lit by paraffin vapour lamps suspended from concrete posts.     *H.B. Priestley*

Collingbourne station, looking south towards Andover. The 2-road goods yard was entered just beyond the up (right hand) platform. The station master's house can be seen in the right background.     *Lens of Sutton*

Weyhill, looking towards Andoversford on 12th August, 1959. There was, at one time, a footbridge here, but this was subsequently removed, and passengers thereafter crossed the line by means of the barrow crossing.                                    *H.B. Priestley*

The standard Gloucester Wagon Company signal box at Weyhill had 20 levers (including spares).                                                                      *H.C. Casserley*

the usual M&SWJ characteristics; there was a hip-roofed station building, a small waiting shelter on the opposite platform, and a Gloucester Wagon Company signal box with 20 levers.

Weyhill village was famous in the past for its annual six day agricultural fair, which was held in October and contributed valuable extra traffic for the railway. Edwardian editions of *The Little Guide to Hampshire* reveal that the fair was, at that time, 'still a fair of great celebrity for sheep, horses, hops and cheese', and it is amusing to recall that this annual event once prompted a bitter argument between the M&SWJ and GWR companies — the origins of the dispute being the rates to be charged for the carriage of hurdles!

### Andover Junction

Midland & South Western Junction metals finally ended at Red Post Junction, which was zero point for milepost distances and was said to derive its name from the boundary mark. From there the company's trains ran over the independent third road, the property of the L&SWR, into Andover Junction station, where the outer face of an island platform on the north side was reserved for them, though incoming trains could use also the up main platform. The distance throughout from Cheltenham to Andover Junction was 69 miles 32 chains.

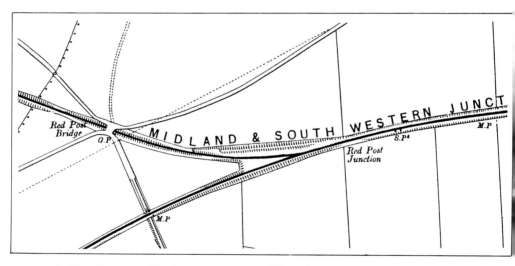

Red Post Junction. This junction was remodelled after 1917.
*Reproduced from the 6", 1911 Ordnance Survey map*

The LSWR and MSWJ sheds at Andover Junction, photographed on 30th April, 1928. The MSWJR shed was the one on the right and Andover Junction station can be glimpsed in the right distance. *H.C. Casserley*

'57XX' class 0−6−0PT No. 9672 stands in Andoversford Junction station with the 2.50 pm train to Swindon on 24th August, 1959. *H.B. Priestley*

# The Tidworth Branch

D.S. Barrie

The MSWJ on Salisbury Plain. A Troop Train seen at Ludgershall around 1900.

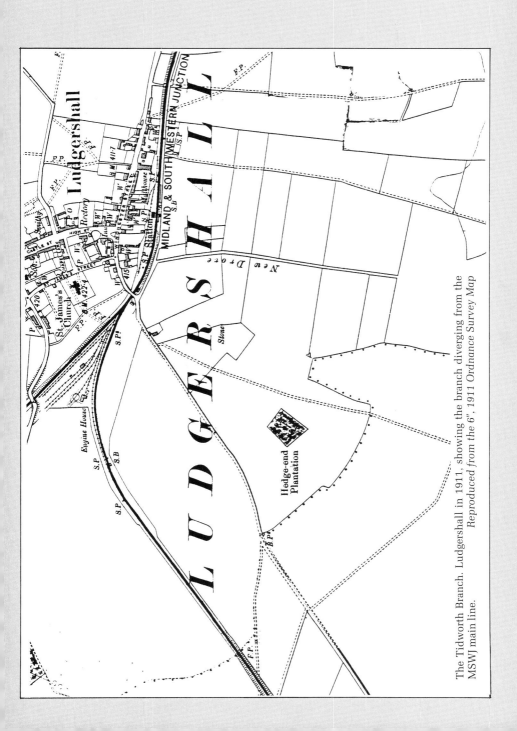

The Tidworth Branch. Ludgershall in 1911, showing the branch diverging from the MSWJ main line. Reproduced from the 6", 1911 Ordnance Survey Map

The wide platforms at Ludgershall were clearly designed to accommodate large numbers of soldiers (including cavalry units); there were few impediments to get in the way during loading or unloading operations, although the resulting station was a bleak and windswept place for ordinary travellers. *Lens of Sutton*

Another view of the spacious platform at Ludgershall, on 1st September, 1952.
*H.C. Casserley*

A panoramic view of Ludgershall goods yard seen from the road overbridge at the western end of the station; the MSWJ main line to Andoversford is on the right, and the Tidworth branch curves away to the left. *Mowat Collection*

Ludgershall station, looking east from the footbridge. The hip-roofed station building was an enlarged version of the MSWJ 'standard' design. *Douglas Thompson*

"WORKMEN'S MAIL." [*W. H. Jones, Ludgershall.*

A fine view of the 'Workmen's mail' seen here just outside Tidworth station. This was carrying the men employed on the building of the new army camp. Note the MSWJ brake vans each end of the contractor's open wagons. The line in the foreground is the branch curving to the barracks. *R.W. Kidner Collection*

Ludgershall station seen in August 1959. *H.B. Priestley*

The South Midlands Brigade disembarking at the main platform at Ludgershall. The cross marks the RAMC camp from which the sender sent the postcard in 1910. The four coach Tidworth branch set can be seen standing in the bay at the left. The coaches on the nearer train appear to be the Swindon Marlborough and Andover stock of 1881 and 1882, having been refitted by the Metropolitan Carriage and Wagon Co.

R.W. Kidner Collection

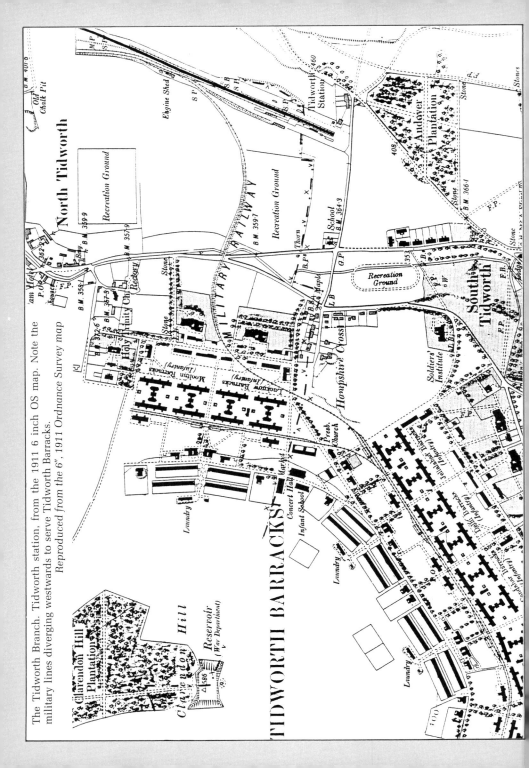

The Tidworth Branch. Tidworth station, from the 1911 6 inch OS map. Note the military lines diverging westwards to serve Tidworth Barracks. Reproduced from the 6", 1911 Ordnance Survey map

The only known view of the branch railway in Lucknor Barracks at Tidworth.

*R.W. Kidner Collection*

The July 1915 Timetable for the Tidworth Branch and Swindon/Chiseldon service.

# LUDGERSHALL & TIDWORTH BRANCH.

## WEEK DAYS.

| | a.m. | a.m. | a.m. | a.m. | a.m. | p.m. | p.m. | p.m. | | p.m. | p.m. | | p.m. | | p.m. | | | p.m. |
|---|---|---|---|---|---|---|---|---|---|---|---|---|---|---|---|---|---|---|
| Tidworth............dep. | 7 0 | 7 38 | 8 47 | 9 45 | 10 55 | 12 15 | *10 25* | 2 35 | ... | 4 10 | 5 *c 0* | ... | 5 15 | ... | 7 35 | ... | ... | *10 15* |
| Ludgershall ...... arr. | 7 7 | 7 44 | 8 53 | 9 51 | 11 1 | 12 22 | *10 32* | 2 41 | ... | 4 16 | 5 *0 7* | ... | 5 21 | ... | 7 41 | ... | ... | *10 22* |
| Weyhill ............ ,, | ... | 7 52 | ... | 10 13 | ... | ... | *10 39* | ... | ... | ... | ... | ... | 5 48 | ... | 8 17 | ... | ... | ... |
| Andover Junct. ... arr. | ... | 7 59 | ... | 10 3 | ... | 12 34 | *10 47* | 2 53 | ... | 4 28 | ... | ... | 5 55 | ... | 8 24 | ... | ... | *10 35* |

| | a.m. | a.m. | a.m. | a.m. | a.m. | a.m. | p.m. | p.m. | p.m. | p.m. | p.m. | p.m. | | p.m. | p.m. | p.m. | p.m. | mid't. |
|---|---|---|---|---|---|---|---|---|---|---|---|---|---|---|---|---|---|---|
| Andover Junct. ...dep. | ... | 7 0 | 8 5 | 8 45 | *Mixd* | 10 56 | 11 10 | 12 20 | 1 5 | *2c 5* | 3 10 | 4 55 | 10 | ... | 7 40 | 7 50 | ... | *10 15* | ... |
| Weyhill ............ ,, | ... | 7 8 | 8 12 | 8 52 | ... | .. | ... | 12 30 | ... | *20 12* | 3 18 | 4 13 | 5 18 | ... | ... | 8 0 | ... | ... |
| Ludgershall ...... ,, | ... | 7 22 | 8 20 | 9 2 | 10 20 | 11 24 | 11 24 | 12 45 | 1 19 | *20 20* | 3 35 | 4 22 | 5 45 | ... | 7 52 | 8 15 | 9 *055* | *11c 2* | *12c 16* |
| Tidworth............ arr. | ... | 7 28 | 8 27 | 9 8 | 10 30 | 11 30 | 11 30 | 12 52 | 1 25 | *20 26* | 3 41 | 4 28 | 5 51 | ... | 8 0 | 8 21 | *10 c 2* | *11c 9* | *12c 22* |

c—Saturdays only.   s— Saturdays excepted.

## SUNDAYS.

| | a.m. | a.m. | a.m. | p.m. | p.m. | p.m. | m'n't. | m'n't. | | | a.m. | a.m. | a.m. | p.m. | | p.m. | p.m. |
|---|---|---|---|---|---|---|---|---|---|---|---|---|---|---|---|---|---|
| Andover Junct. dep. | ... | 10 36 | 11 30 | 6 25 | 8 25 | 8 35 | 12 12 | 12 23 | Tidworth......dep. | | 8 45 | 1035 | 11 35 | 5 40 | ... | 8 25 | 9 5 |
| Weyhill ......... ,, | ... | ... | 11 39 | ... | 8 33 | ... | ... | ... | Ludgershall ... arr. | | 8 51 | 1041 | 11 42 | 5 46 | ... | 8 32 | 9 12 |
| Ludgershall .. ,, | 9 5 | 10 52 | 11 47 | 7 8 | 8 45 | 8 55 | 12 30 | 12 40 | Weyhill ...... ,, | | 9 10 | ... | ... | ... | ... | | |
| Tidworth......... arr. | 9 12 | 10 58 | | 7 15 | 8 52 | 9 5 | 12 37 | 12 50 | Andover Junct. ,, | | 9 20 | ... | ... | 6 4 | | | |

# TRAIN SERVICE—SWINDON TOWN & CHISELDON.

## WEEK DAYS.

| | a.m | a.m. | a.m. | p.m. | p m. | p.m. | p.m. | p.m. | p.m. | p.m. | p.m. | p.m. | p.m. | p.m. | | |
|---|---|---|---|---|---|---|---|---|---|---|---|---|---|---|---|---|
| Swindon Town dep. | 5 5 | 6 55 | 9 5 | *1815* | 2*s* 0 | 2 35 | 2*s45* | 4 40 | 6 0 | 6 45 | 8*s30* | 8 50 | 10*s* | 0 *11s* 0 | *11s20* | ... | ... |
| Chiseldon ... arr. | 5 12 | 7 1 | 9 12 | *1822* | 2*s* 7 | 2 41 | 2*s52* | 4 47 | 6 7 | 6 52 | 8*s37* | 8 57 | 10*s* 7 | *11s* 7 | *11s27* | ... | ... |

| | a.m. | a.m. | a.m. | p.m. | p.m. | p.m. | p.m. | p.m. | p.m. | p.m. | p.m. | p.m. | | |
|---|---|---|---|---|---|---|---|---|---|---|---|---|---|---|
| Chiseldon ... dep. | 5 20 | 8 16 | 9 53 | *1830* | 1 50 | 2*s20* | 3*s25* | 4 20 | 6*s 8* | 6 22 | 6*s30* | 9*s15* | 9 26 | *10s20* | ... | ... |
| Swindon Town arr. | 5 27 | 8 22 | 9 59 | *1837* | 1 57 | 2*s27* | 3*s32* | 4 27 | 6*s14* | 6 28 | 6*s36* | 9*s22* | 9 33 | *10s27* | ... | ... |

s—Saturdays only.

## SUNDAYS.

| | a.m. | p.m. | p.m. | p.m. | p.m. | p.m. | p.m. | p.m. | | | p.m. | p.m. | p.m. | p.m. | p.m. | p.m. | p.m. |
|---|---|---|---|---|---|---|---|---|---|---|---|---|---|---|---|---|---|
| Swindon Town dep. | 7 50 | 2 10 | 2 45 | 4 50 | 6 0 | 6 50 | 8 30 | Chiseldon ... dep. | | 1 0 | 2 30 | 3 37 | 7 12 | 7 20 | 9 0 | 9 37 |
| Chiseldon ... arr. | 7 57 | 2 17 | 2 51 | 4 57 | 6 7 | 6 57 | 8 37 | Swindon Town arr. | | 1 8 | 2 37 | 3 43 | 7 19 | 7 27 | 9 7 | 9 43 |

A fine view of Tidworth station in 1906. The 0–6–0T No. 13 is seen arriving with the 'Tidworth set'. This comprised four, six-wheeled carriages which only worked the branch.

*R.W. Kidner Collection*

A general view of Tidworth station looking south towards the terminal buffer stops in 1928; like Ludgershall, Tidworth was designed to accommodate large numbers of soldiers at any one time. *Mowat Collection*

Tidworth, looking north towards Ludgershall, with the standard MSWJ style station buildings visible to the left. *Douglas Thompson*

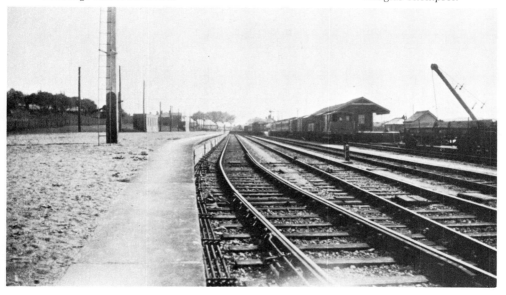

### Southern Command
# TIDWORTH TATTOO

IN THE
## Arena, Tidworth Park, Tidworth, Hants
#### (TIDWORTH STATION ADJOINS THE PARK)

## SATURDAYS, JULY 30th, and AUGUST 6th, and MONDAY, TUESDAY, WEDNESDAY, THURSDAY and FRIDAY, AUGUST 1st, 2nd, 3rd, 4th, and 5th.

# EXCURSIONS
TO
# TIDWORTH

| LEAVING | Sat., July 30th, at | Mon., Aug. 1st, at | Tues., Aug. 2nd, at | Wed., Aug. 3rd, at | Thurs., Aug. 4th, at | Fri., Aug. 5th, at | Sat., Aug. 6th, at | RETURN FARES. | |
|---|---|---|---|---|---|---|---|---|---|
| | p.m. | p.m. | p.m. | p.m. | p.m. | p.m. | p.m. | s. | d. |
| SWINDON JUNCTION | 6 55 | — | 6 55 | 6 50 | 6 40 | — | 6 55 | 7 0 | } 2 8 |
| SWINDON TOWN | 7 5 | — | 7 5 | 7 5 | — | 7 5 | 7 5 | — 6 15 | |
| CHISELDON | 7 15 | — | 7 15 | 7 15 | — | 7 20 | 7 15 | — 6 25 | |
| CHISELDON CAMP H. | 7 20 | — | — | — | — | — | — | — | } 2 1 |
| OGBOURNE | 7 25 | — | — | — | — | — | 7 25 | — 6 35 | |
| MARLBOROUGH | 7 35 | — | 7 35 | 7 35 | — | 7 45 | 7 35 | — 6 45 | 1 7 |
| SAVERNAKE (H.L.) | 7 50 | 7 50 | 7 50 | 7 45 | — | 7 55 | 7 50 | — 6 55 | 1 4 |
| GRAFTON AND BURBAGE | 7 55 | 7 55 | 7 55 | — | — | — | 7 55 | — 7 5 | 1 1 |
| COLLINGBOURNE KINGSTON HALT | — | — | — | — | — | — | — | 7 10 | 1 0 |
| COLLINGBOURNE | 8 10 | 8 5 | 8 5 | 8 0 | — | 8 15 | 8 10 | — 7 15 | 0 9½ |
| LUDGERSHALL | 8 20 | 8 20 | 8 20 | 8 10 | — | 8 25 | 8 20 | — 7 30 | 0 5½ |
| TIDWORTH .. arr. | 8 30 | 8 30 | 8 30 | 8 25 | 8 25 | 8 40 | 8 30 | 8 25 7 40 | 3rd CLASS. |

### RETURN ARRANGEMENTS.

RETURN TRAINS will leave TIDWORTH as under :—

SATURDAY, JULY 30th.—To ALL BOOKING STATIONS at 1.10 a.m. (early Sunday morning).

MONDAY, AUGUST 1st.—To ALL BOOKING STATIONS at 12.40 a.m. (early Tuesday morning).

TUESDAY, AUGUST 2nd.—To ALL BOOKING STATIONS at 1.50 a.m. (early Wednesday morning).

WEDNESDAY, AUGUST 3rd.—To ALL BOOKING STATIONS at 2.10 a.m. (early Thursday morning).

THURSDAY, AUGUST 4th.—To SWINDON JUNCTION at 2.0 a.m. (early Friday morning). To ALL OTHER BOOKING STATIONS at 2.10 a.m. (early Friday morning).

FRIDAY, AUGUST 5th.—To ALL BOOKING STATIONS at 1.0 a.m. (early Saturday morning).

SATURDAY, AUGUST 6th.—To SWINDON JUNCTION at 1.0 a.m. (early Sunday morning). To ALL OTHER BOOKING STATIONS at 2.0 a.m. (early Sunday morning).

| RETURN FARES. | | LEAVING | Sats., Mon., Tues., Wed., Thurs. and Fri., July 30, Aug. 1, 2, 3, 4, 5 & 6. | RETURN FARES. | |
|---|---|---|---|---|---|
| s. | d. | | p.m. | s. | d. |
| 1 | 1 | ANDOVER JUNCTION | 7 43 | 1 | 1 |
| 1 | 0 | WEYHILL | 7 50 | 1 | 0 |
| THIRD CLASS. | | TIDWORTH .. arr. | 8 10 | THIRD CLASS. | |

Change at Ludgershall on forward journey only.

### RETURN ARRANGEMENTS.

RETURN TRAINS will leave TIDWORTH as under :—

SATURDAY, JULY 30th.—At 12.30 a.m. (early Sunday morning).
MONDAY, AUGUST 1st.—At 1.0 a.m. (early Tuesday morning).
TUESDAY, AUGUST 2nd.—At 12.50 a.m. (early Wednesday morning).
WEDNESDAY, AUGUST 3rd.—At 12.40 a.m. (early Thursday morning).
THURSDAY, AUGUST 4th.—At 1.20 a.m. (early Friday morning).
FRIDAY, AUGUST 5th.—At 1.10 a.m. (early Saturday morning).
SATURDAY, AUGUST 6th.—At 1.20 a.m. (early Sunday morning).

### TATTOO ADMISSION TICKETS.

A LIMITED NUMBER OF TATTOO ADMISSION TICKETS ARE OBTAINABLE AT THE BOOKING STATIONS. FOR FULL PARTICULARS, SEE OTHER SIDE.

TAKE YOUR TICKETS IN ADVANCE.

A 1930s Handbill for the Tidworth Tattoo.

# Chapter Five

# The Years of Decline

The 1914–18 war left Britain's railways in a run-down condition, and it was decided that the national interest would best be served if the independent companies that controlled much of the British transport system were 'grouped' into four large undertakings. The Railways Act of 1921 provided for the setting up of a 'Railways Tribunal' which would supervise the proposed grouping, and in May 1922 *The Railway Magazine* reported that the first scheme laid before the tribunal had been for the amalgamation of the Cambrian, the Cardiff, the Taff Vale and other Welsh companies with the GWR. Preliminary schemes for the inclusion of certain English minor lines within the GWR group had also been approved, but there was — significantly — no mention of the Midland & South Western Junction Railway.

## The End of the M&SWJ Company

It was, perhaps, understandable that the M&SWJ should have resisted an amalgamation with the Great Western, and the little company presented something of a problem for the Railway Tribunal. Indeed the matter was not settled until the very *last* sitting of the tribunal on 28th September, 1923, when the M&SWJ case was finally settled 'without difficulty'; it was, by that time, clear to all concerned that the Midland & South Western Junction Railway would become a mere appendage of the GWR.

It may seem surprising that it should have fallen to the lot of the M&SWJ to be absorbed under the Railways Act, 1921, by its traditional enemy, the GWR, but it could hardly have been otherwise. The interests of the Midland and L&SWR did not approach legal ownership, and thus the M&SWJ was never a 'joint' railway. Moreover, a line so deeply embedded in GWR territory could not have passed into other hands without violence to long-standing agreements — statutory in the case of the Midland.

The last Chairman of the company was S. J. Portal, son of a former Chairman of the L&SWR. Others who had occupied the chair included two Marquesses of Ailesbury, E. W. Cripps, of Cirencester, and F. C. Scotter, son of Sir Charles Scotter, a former General Manager and Chairman of the L&SWR, and a partner in the stockbroking firm of Mortimer, Scotter & Co., which had played a leading part in financing the Marlborough & Grafton Railway.

The normal complement of the Board was nine, representative of debenture holders (five), preference holders (two) and ordinary shareholders (two). Many prominent local people had served from time to time, such as A. L. Goddard, of Swindon, Lord Bathurst (Cirencester), and W. E. Nicolson Browne of Chiseldon. The last-named, a stalwart on the Board for 32 years continuously from 1873 until his death in 1905, gave unstinted service to the company, especially in the difficult months preceding Fay's appointment as General Manager, which he did much to bring about. He was, among other things, coroner for North Wilts. and when the fortunes of the M&SWJ were at their lowest ebb he had put up with wholly undeserved gibes from shareholders, comparing his attendance at meetings of the company with his attendance on 'other dead bodies'. Sir William Acworth, the well-known railway economist and author of *The Railways of England*, was a Director from 1905 to 1923.

## Post-Grouping Developments

The post-grouping era was not a happy one for the former Midland & South Western Junction Railway. Old animosities died hard, and a company that had survived very largely by filching traffic from its neighbour could scarcely hope to find a ready niche in that neighbour's household. The change of regime brought some advantages. The passenger service between Swindon Town and Swindon main line station was restored on 22nd October, 1923; the wear and tear of the war years was made good; and the strengthening of weak bridges, put in hand in 1930, enabled the line to carry heavy locomotives in the GWR 'blue' route category.

The grouping brought some other positive developments, notably the new halts that were opened at Chiseldon Camp and Collingbourne Kingston on 1st December, 1930 and 1st April, 1932 respectively. Furthermore, a complicated but sensible rearrangement of the layout between Marlborough and Wolfhall Junction, completed and brought into use on 6th March, 1933, made it possible to close the terminal passenger station at Marlborough with part of the original GWR branch from Savernake and to concentrate all passenger traffic at the former M&SWJ station. In a renaming of stations the M&SWJ station became Marlborough (Low Level) on 1st July, 1924, but at Savernake the position was reversed; there the M&SWJ station became the High Level and the GWR station the Low Level. Meanwhile, Cirencester (M&SWJ) became Cirencester Watermoor* to prevent confusion with the nearby GWR terminus, which henceforth became Cirencester Town.

On the debit side, the line between Andoversford Junction and Cirencester was reduced to single track in 1928, and the train service steadily deteriorated, until the M&SWJ route had become little more than a sluggish backwater.

In the early post-grouping period, traffic on the Midland & South Western Junction line was still handled by former M&SWJ 4−4−0s and 0−6−0s, but when several of these engines were sent away for rebuilding, Great Western 'Duke' class 4−4−0s were sent as replacements. Small-wheeled '45XX' class 2−6−2Ts and Dean Goods 0−6−0s also appeared in the post-1923 period — indeed, Dean Goods No. 2355 was sent to Cirencester for overhaul in order to provide some work while so many M&SWJ engines were being rebuilt at Swindon.

Sadly, few of the older Midland & South Western Junction locomotives remained for long in their native territory; they were either scrapped or sent elsewhere after rebuilding. Exceptions were the unrebuilt Sharp Stewart 4−4−4T (GWR No. 25) and the Beyer Peacock 0−4−4T (GWR No. 23), both of which worked between Swindon Town and Swindon Junction for a few years.

After completion of the bridge-strengthening programme in the early 1930s, the remaining Midland & South Western Junction engines were

---

* The station was known as Watermoor before 1923, but tickets, etc., referred to 'Cirencester M&SWJ', and Cirencester Watermoor only came into general usage after the grouping.

## CHELTENHAM SPA, SWINDON, TIDWORTH, and ANDOVER

| Down | | Week Days. | | Sundays. |
|---|---|---|---|---|

(Timetable grid — stations and times for Down services)

Stations include: 656 Bradford (ForsterSq.) dp, 656 Leeds (City), 656 York, 656 Sheffield (L.M.S.), 656 Liverpool (Central), 656 (Lime St.), 656 Manchester (Central), 656 (Lon. Rd.), 656 Derby (L.M.S.), 656 Birmingham (New St.), 656 Worcester (S.E.) ...

Cheltenham Spa A dep, Cheltenham (South) B, Charlton Kings, Andoversford Junction, Withington (Glos), Chedworth, Foss Cross, Cirencester C 92, South Cerney, Cricklade, Swindon Town arr.

Blunsdon, Swindon Town, Swindon Town dep., Chiseldon, Ogbourne, Marlborough, Savernake (Low Level) F 2, 8, Grafton and Burbage, Collingbourne, Ludgershall, Ludgershall dep., Tidworth, Ludgershall arr., Weyhill, Andover J. 176, 189, 189 Southampton Cen. arr., 189 Southampton H, 184 Portsmouth H, 154 Bournemouth Cen., 170 Salisbury, 173 London (Waterloo)

Bradshaw's timetable for July 1939.

## ANDOVER, TIDWORTH, SWINDON, and CHELTENHAM SPA

| Up. | | Week Days. | | Sundays. |
|---|---|---|---|---|

(Timetable grid — stations and times for Up services)

Stations include: 170 London (Waterloo) dep., 173 Salisbury, 159 Bournemouth Cen., 187 Portsmouth H, 189 Southampton Ter., 189 Southampton Cen.

Andover Junction dep., Weyhill, Ludgershall arr., Ludgershall dep., Tidworth, Ludgershall dep., Collingbourne, Grafton and Burbage, Savernake (Low Level) F 2, 8, Marlborough, Ogbourne, Chiseldon, Swindon Town arr., Swindon Town 54, 64 dep., Swindon Town dep., Cricklade, South Cerney, Cirencester C 92, Foss Cross, Chedworth, Withington (Glos), Andoversford Junction, Charlton Kings, Cheltenham (South) B 660, Cheltenham Spa A 136 arr., 660 Worcester (S.E.) arr., 660 Birmingham (New St.), 660 Derby (L.M.S.), 660 Manchester (Lon. Rd.), 660 (Central), 660 Liverpool (Lime St.), 660 (Central), 660 Sheffield (L.M.S.), 660 York, 660 Leeds (City), 660 Bradford (ForsterSq.)

A Landsdown. B Cheltenham (South) & Leckhampton. C Watermoor. E Except Sats. F Change at Southampton Cen. H Portsmouth & Southsea. K Change at Eastleigh and Romsey. P Stops to take up only. Z Change at Eastleigh and Romsey. S Sats only. Yy Stops at 6 10 aft to take up only.

¶ "Halts" at Collingbourne Kingston between Collingbourne and Grafton & Burbage; and at Chiseldon Camp, between Ogbourne and Chiseldon.

**OTHER TRAINS** between Tidworth & Ludgershall, 78—Savernake & Marlborough, 50—Andoversford and Cheltenham Spa, 136.

gradually replaced by Great Western '43XX' class 2−6−0s, Collett '2251' class 0−6−0s, and large prairies of the '51XX' class, while '28XX' class 2−8−0s occasionally appeared at the head of heavy freight trains. Loco-motives in greater variety, including 'Grange' and 'Manor' 4−6−0s and Southern Railway 2−6−0s and 'T9' 4−4−0s, appeared at the height of each summer season on special trains conveying cadets to and from annual camps on Salisbury Plain, and on long-distance excursions to Tidworth for the Military Tattoo, which achieved immense popularity in the years preceding World War II.

Dean clerestories and other Great Western vehicles were used on the M&SWJ line in increasing numbers after 1923, and many trains were formed of both GWR and former Midland & South Western Junction coaches; the latter were repainted in standard Great Western chocolate and cream livery, but could be distinguished, even from a distance, by their low arc-roofs.

## World War II

Although the 1920s and 1930s must be seen as a time of relative decline for the Midland & South Western Junction line, the route came into its own again during the dark days of World War II, and for six or seven years the M&SWJ carried a flood of military traffic.

Pre-war assessments of the likely effects of mass bombing had predicted that London and other urban centres would be rapidly knocked-out by a series of massive air raids, and faced with this dreadful scenario (which was so appalling that it remained secret throughout the war) the government identified certain key supply routes between the Midlands and Channel ports such as Dover and Southampton. One of these vital routes was the former Midland & South Western Junction Railway which, being well away from London (and other prime targets) was an ideal military supply route.

In the event, the Whitehall 'experts' who had forecast 2 million British casualties in the first six months of war had seriously over-estimated the destructive capabilities of the *Luftwaffe*, and London's rail links were never destroyed. Nevertheless, the Midland & South Western Junction line played its part as a short-cut between Southampton and the Midlands, while at the same time the route served a variety of aerodromes and military establish-ments in the surrounding area. Savernake Forest, for example, was turned into a vast ammunition dump, served by a nest of sidings entered from the main line about two miles north of Savernake (High Level) station. During the steady build-up of forces for the Normandy landings in 1944, troops, weapons, and stores poured into the military areas on the Marlborough Downs and near Tidworth, and signal boxes along the route were open day and night continuously.

The heavy wartime traffic of the years 1939 to 1945 was handled by a variety of locomotive types, including Stanier 2−8−0s and Ministry of Supply engines, as well as the familiar Great Western passenger and freight classes.

In physical terms, the exigencies of war gave rise to several changes and improvements to the line between Andoversford and Andover; the widening

**Table 115 CHELTENHAM SPA, SWINDON, TIDWORTH, and ANDOVER JUNCTION**

| Miles | Week Days | a.m | a.m | a.m | a.m | p.m | a.m | a.m | | p.m | p.m | p.m | p.m | p.m | p.m | p.m | p.m | p.m | Suns. a.m | Suns. p.m |
|---|---|---|---|---|---|---|---|---|---|---|---|---|---|---|---|---|---|---|---|---|
| | | Except Saturdays | | | | Saturdays only | TC Cheltenham Spa (Lansdown) to Southampton (Central and Terminus) | | Saturdays only; Sats. only | Except Saturdays | Saturdays only | TC Cheltenham Spa (Lansdown) to Southampton (Central and Ter.) | Except Saturdays | | | | Except Saturdays | | | |
| — | Cheltenham Spa A dep | .. | .. | .. | .. | .. | 10 5 | .. | | | .. | 2 3 | .. | 3 20 | .. | .. | | 8 0 | .. | .. |
| 2 | Cheltenham (South) B | .. | .. | 6 36 | .. | .. | 10 10 | 1044 | | | 1218 | 2 8 | 2 54 | 3 25 | 5 53 | 7 18 | | 8 5 | .. | .. |
| 3¼ | Charlton Kings | .. | .. | 6 41 | .. | .. | 10 15 | 1048 | | | 1223 | .. | 2 59 | 3 30 | 5 58 | 7 23 | | 8 10 | .. | .. |
| 7 | Andoversford Junction | .. | .. | 6 50 | .. | .. | 10 26 | 1057 | | | 1232 | 2 20 | 3 8 | 3 40 | 6 7 | 7 32 | | 8 20 | .. | .. |
| 9¾ | Withington (Glos.) | | .. | Stop | .. | .. | 10 33 | .. | | | Stop | .. | Stop | 3 45 | Stop | Stop | | 8 26 | .. | .. |
| 13¼ | Chedworth | | .. | | .. | .. | 10 42 | .. | | | | .. | | 3 55 | | | | 8 35 | .. | .. |
| 14¼ | Foss Cross | | .. | .. | .. | .. | 10 48 | .. | | | .. | .. | .. | 3 58 | .. | .. | | 8 40 | .. | .. |
| 20¼ | Cirencester C | | 6E34 | .. | .. | .. | 11 2 | .. | | | .. | 2 48 | .. | 4 10 | .. | .. | 7 5 | 8 53 | .. | .. |
| 23¼ | South Cerney | | 6E40 | .. | .. | .. | 11 10 | .. | | | .. | .. | .. | 4 19 | .. | .. | 7 11 | 9 0 | .. | .. |
| 27¼ | Cricklade | | 6E49 | .. | .. | .. | 11 20 | .. | | | .. | 3 0 | .. | 4 30 | .. | .. | 7 24 | 9 8 | .. | .. |
| 35¼ | Swindon Town arr | | 7E3 | .. | .. | .. | 11 37 | .. | | | p.m | 3 15 | .. | 4 45 | p.m | p.m | 7 39 | 9 25 | .. | .. |
| — | Mls Swindon dep | | .. | .. | 8 20 | .. | 11 13 | .. | 1224 | 1 5 | 1 6 | .. | | 4 20 | 5E50 | 6 30 | .. | .. | 10 20 | 4 55 |
| — | 3 Swindon Town arr | | .. | a.m | 8 30 | .. | 11 21 | .. | 1232 | 1 13 | 1 13 | .. | | 4 28 | 5E58 | 6 40 | .. | .. | 10 28 | 5 5 |
| — | Swindon Town dep | 6 41 | 7 20 | 8 9 | 8 35 | | 11 42 | .. | 1234 | 1 14 | 1 15 | 3 18 | | 4 48 | 6 0 | 6 41 | .. | 9 30 | 10 30 | 5 10 |
| 39 | Chiseldon | 6 49 | 7 29 | 8 17 | 8 43 | | 11 53 | .. | 1243 | 1 22 | 1 24 | 3 27 | | 4 57 | 6 9 | 6 50 | .. | 9 38 | 10 40 | 5 18 |
| 40¼ | Chiseldon Camp Halt | .. | 7 33 | Stop | 8 46 | | .. | .. | Stop | .. | 1 28 | 3 30 | | 5 0 | .. | 6 53 | .. | 9 43 | 10 44 | 5 23 |
| 42¼ | Ogbourne | .. | 7 39 | | 8 52 | | 12 2 | .. | | .. | 1 35 | 3 38 | | 5 6 | .. | 6 59 | .. | 9 49 | 10 50 | 5 29 |
| 47¼ | Marlborough | .. | 7 53 | .. | 9 5 | | 12 15 | .. | .. | .. | 1Y49 | 3 50 | | 5 17 | .. | 7 11 | .. | 10 1 | 11 1 | 5 39 |
| 52¼ | Savernake (Low Level) F | .. | 8 5 | .. | 9k32 | | 12T27 | .. | .. | .. | 2 16 | 4T1 | | 5T29 | .. | 7R26 | .. | 10T13 | 11T12 | 5T51 |
| 54¼ | Grafton and Burbage | .. | .. | .. | 9 38 | | .. | .. | .. | .. | | 4 6 | | 5 36 | .. | 7 33 | .. | 10 20 | 11 18 | 5 57 |
| 58 | Collingbourne Kingston | .. | .. | .. | 9 44 | | 12P36 | .. | .. | .. | | 4 11 | | 5 41 | .. | 7 38 | .. | 10 26 | 11 22 | 6 3 |
| 58½ | Collingbourne [Halt | .. | .. | .. | 9 48 | | 12P39 | .. | .. | .. | | 4 14 | | 5 45 | .. | 7 42 | .. | 10 30 | 11 26 | 6 8 |
| 61 | Ludgershall arr | .. | .. | .. | 9 54 | | 12 42 | .. | p.m | .. | | 4 20 | | 5 51 | .. | 7 48 | .. | 10 36 | 11 32 | 6 14 |
| — | Ludgershall dep | .. | .. | .. | 10 18 | .. | 12E50 | .. | 1 35 | .. | | 4 25 | | 6 0 | .. | 8 5 | .. | .. | .. | .. |
| 63½ | Tidworth arr | .. | .. | a.m | 10 25 | .. | 1E0 | .. | 1 45 | .. | | 4 32 | p.m | 6 7 | .. | 8 12 | .. | .. | .. | .. |
| | Tidworth dep | .. | .. | 8 45 | .. | 1225 | 12 25 | .. | | .. | | 3 55 | 5 12 | 5 12 | .. | 7 30 | .. | .. | .. | .. |
| — | Ludgershall arr | .. | .. | 8 52 | .. | 1232 | 12 32 | .. | | .. | | 4 2 | 5 19 | 5 19 | .. | 7 37 | .. | .. | .. | .. |
| — | Ludgershall dep | .. | .. | 8 53 | 9 57 | 1233 | 12 43 | .. | | .. | | 4 21 | 5 20 | 5 52 | .. | 7 51 | .. | 10 37 | 11 34 | 6 15 |
| 65 | Weyhill | .. | .. | 9 1 | 10 5 | 1241 | .. | .. | | .. | | 4 29 | 5 27 | 6 0 | .. | 7 59 | .. | 10 45 | 11 42 | 6 22 |
| 68½ | Andover Junction arr | .. | .. | 9 9 | 10 13 | 1249 | 1 0 | .. | | .. | | 4 37 | 5 35 | 6 8 | .. | 8 7 | .. | 10 53 | 11 50 | 6 30 |
| 94½ | Southern Region: SOUTHAMPTON C. arr | .. | .. | 10l47 | 12 40 | .. | 2 10 | .. | | .. | | 5 42 | .. | 7 41 | .. | 10Z48 | .. | .. | 2Z8 | 8 12 |
| 96½ | SOUTHAMPTON G " | .. | .. | 10 47 | .. | .. | 2 20 | .. | | .. | | 5 50 | .. | .. | .. | .. | .. | .. | 2Z31 | 8 45 |
| 121 | PORTSMOUTH H " | .. | .. | 11 36 | 2A1 | .. | 3 21 | .. | | .. | | 7 2 | .. | 8 58 | .. | 2aZ28 | .. | .. | 3Z4 | 9 30 |
| 118 | BOURNEMOUTH C. " | .. | .. | 12n13 | 2r22 | .. | 3 40 | .. | | .. | | 7 3 | .. | 8q51 | .. | 2aZ14 | .. | .. | 4Z15 | 9 24 |
| 85¾ | SALISBURY " | .. | .. | 9 58 | 10b55 | .. | 2 19 | .. | | .. | | 6 0 | .. | 7 8 | .. | 9 51 | .. | .. | 12 57 | 9 43 |
| 135 | London (W'loo) " | .. | .. | 11z8 | 12 20 | .. | 3c49 | .. | | .. | | 6d40 | 8 0 | 8 25 | .. | 10 9 | .. | .. | 4 10 | 8 40 |

A Lansdown: about ½ mile to Malvern Road Station and 1 mile to St. James' Station
A Arr. 1 35 p.m. on Fridays and Saturdays (1 8 p.m. on Saturdays 1st July to 9th September)
a a.m.
B Cheltenham (South) and Leckhampton
b Arr. 10 47 a.m. on Saturdays
C Watermoor
C Dep. Derby 10 55 a.m., Birmingham 12 9 and Worcester (S.H.) 12 25 p.m. on Saturdays
c Arr. 2 28 p.m. on Saturdays
d Arr. 6 35 p.m. on Saturdays

E Except Saturdays
F About 250 yards to High Level Station
f Dep. 10 55 p.m. on Fridays
f Dep. Bradford (F.Sq.) 7 45, Leeds (City) 8 28 and Sheffield 9 50 a.m. on Saturdays
G Southampton Terminus for Docks
H Portsmouth and Southsea
k Arr 9 17 a.m.
L Dep. Derby 6 40, Birmingham (N. St.) 8 9 and Worcester (S.H.) 9 8 a.m. on Saturdays
l Arr. 10 50 a.m. on Saturdays
n Arr. 11 35 a.m. on Saturdays
P Stops on Fridays and Saturdays to take up passengers

q Arr. 8 40 p.m. on Fridays
R Arr. Savernake 7 23 p.m. On Saturdays arrive and depart from High Level Station
r Arr. 1 40 p.m. on Saturdays
S Saturdays only
T High Level Station
TC Through Carriages
z Arr. 10 59 a.m. on Saturdays commencing 24th June
Y Dep. 2 5 p.m
y Dep. 8 0 a.m. on Saturdays
Z Via Salisbury

**LOCAL TRAINS** between Marlborough and Savernake, see Table 67

| Miles | Week Days | a.m | a.m | a.m | a.m | a.m | a.m | a.m | a.m | p.m | p.m | p.m | p.m | p.m | p.m | p.m | p.m | p.m | p.m | p.m | p.m |
|---|---|---|---|---|---|---|---|---|---|---|---|---|---|---|---|---|---|---|---|---|---|
| | | Except Saturdays | Except Saturdays | | | | | | Southampton (Terminus and Central) to Cheltenham Spa (Lansdown) | | Except Saturdays | Saturdays only | | | Except Saturdays | | Southampton (Terminus and Central) to Cheltenham Spa (Lansdown) | | | | |
| — | Andover Junction dep | .. | .. | 6 45 | 7 0 | 8 5 | .. | 9 58 | 11 7 | 1 15 | .. | .. | 2 35 | .. | .. | .. | 5 36 | .. | 7 45 | 12 38 | 8 5 |
| 3½ | Weyhill | .. | .. | 6 54 | .. | 8 12 | .. | 10 5 | 11 16 | 1 22 | .. | .. | 2 42 | .. | .. | .. | 5 44 | .. | 7 51 | 12 44 | 8 12 |
| 7½ | Ludgershall arr | .. | .. | 7 3 | 7 15 | 8 20 | .. | 1011 | 11 24 | 1 30 | .. | .. | 2 50 | .. | .. | .. | 5 53 | .. | 7 59 | 12 52 | 8 20 |
| — | Ludgershall dep | .. | .. | 7 5 | .. | 8 30 | .. | 1018 | 11 30 | 1 35 | .. | | 2 57 | .. | .. | .. | 6 0 | .. | 8 5 | .. | .. |
| 9½ | Tidworth arr | .. | .. | 7 12 | .. | 8 37 | .. | 1025 | 11 37 | 1 43 | .. | | 3 4 | .. | .. | .. | 6 7 | .. | 8 12 | .. | .. |
| | Tidworth dep | .. | .. | Stop | .. | 8 5 | .. | Stop | 11 5 | Stop | .. | | 2 35 | .. | .. | .. | 5 12 | .. | 7 30 | .. | .. |
| — | Ludgershall arr | .. | .. | | .. | 8 12 | .. | | 11 12 | | | | 2 42 | .. | .. | .. | 5 19 | .. | 7 37 | .. | .. |
| — | Ludgershall dep | .. | | .. | 7 22 | 8 22 | .. | .. | 11 26 | .. | | | 2 52 | .. | .. | .. | 5 55 | .. | 8 3 | 12 53 | 8 24 |
| 10 | Collingbourne [Halt | .. | | .. | 7 29 | 8 29 | .. | .. | .. | .. | | | 2 58 | .. | .. | .. | 6 1 | .. | 8 8 | 12 59 | 8 30 |
| 10½ | Collingbourne Kingston | .. | | .. | 7 32 | 8 32 | .. | .. | .. | .. | | | 3 1 | .. | | .. | 6 4 | .. | 8 11 | 1 2 | 8 35 |
| 14¼ | Grafton and Burbage | .. | | .. | 7 40 | 8 40 | .. | .. | .. | .. | | | 3 8 | .. | | .. | 6 9 | .. | 8 17 | 1 8 | 8 44 |
| 16¼ | Savernake (Low Level) F | | | .. | 8R22 | 8T49 | .. | .. | 11T41 | .. | | 1255 | 3 16 | .. | | .. | 6T18 | 7 50 | 8S31 | 1T14 | 8T52 |
| 21¼ | Marlborough | | | .. | 8 37 | 9 0 | 9 15 | .. | 11 52 | .. | | 1827 | 3 27 | .. | | .. | 6 30 | 8H4 | 8 42 | 1 26 | 9 4 |
| 26¼ | Ogbourne | | | .. | .. | 9 13 | 9 24 | .. | 12 4 | .. | | 1 40 | 3 37 | .. | | .. | 6 40 | 8 15 | 8 52 | 1 37 | 9 16 |
| 28¼ | Chiseldon Camp Halt | | | a.m | .. | 9 18 | .. | .. | .. | p.m | | 1 46 | 3 42 | .. | | .. | .. | 8 20 | 8 57 | 1 42 | 9 22 |
| 29¾ | Chiseldon | | 6 57 | 8 25 | .. | 9 22 | 9 33 | .. | 12 11 | 12S57 | 1 38 | 1 51 | 3 46 | .. | | 6 20 | 6 50 | 8 25 | 9 2 | 1 47 | 9 27 |
| 32¾ | Swindon Town arr | | 7 5 | 8 33 | .. | 9 31 | 9 43 | .. | 12 19 | 1S5 | 1 46 | 2 0 | 3 55 | .. | | 6 27 | 7 2 | 8 35 | 9 11 | 1 56 | 9 36 |
| — | Swindon Town dep | | 7 3 | Stop | .. | .. | 9 52 | .. | 12 38 | Stop | 1 47 | 2 4 | .. | 5 22 | .. | .. | .. | Stop | 9 13 | 1 58 | 9 38 |
| 35½ | Swindon arr | | 7 15 | | .. | .. | 10 1 | .. | 12 47 | | 1 55 | 2 14 | .. | 5 30 | .. | .. | .. | | 9 23 | 2 8 | 9 47 |
| — | Swindon Town dep | 5 45 | .. | .. | .. | 9 37 | .. | .. | 12 22 | .. | .. | .. | 4 0 | Stop | 6 5 | .. | 7 5 | .. | Stop | .. | .. |
| 41½ | Cricklade | 6 0 | .. | .. | .. | 9 52 | .. | .. | 12 37 | .. | .. | .. | 4 13 | | 6 20 | .. | 7 22 | .. | | .. | .. |
| 44½ | South Cerney | 6 8 | .. | .. | .. | 10 0 | .. | .. | 12S44 | .. | .. | .. | 4 20 | .. | 6 28 | .. | 7 29 | .. | .. | .. | .. |
| 47½ | Cirencester C | 6 15 | .. | .. | .. | 10 10 | .. | .. | 12 52 | .. | .. | .. | 4 30 | .. | 6 35 | .. | 7 33 | .. | .. | .. | .. |
| 54 | Foss Cross | .. | .. | .. | .. | 10 21 | .. | .. | .. | .. | .. | .. | 4 42 | .. | .. | .. | .. | .. | .. | .. | .. |
| 55 | Chedworth | .. | .. | .. | .. | 10 25 | .. | .. | .. | .. | .. | .. | 4 46 | .. | .. | .. | 7 52 | .. | .. | .. | .. |
| 58½ | Withington (Glos.) | .. | .. | a.m | .. | 10 33 | .. | p.m | .. | p.m. | .. | .. | 4 54 | p.m | .. | .. | 7 59 | p.m | p.m | .. | .. |
| 61½ | Andoversford Junction | .. | .. | 8 30 | .. | 10 40 | .. | 1251 | .. | 2 14 | .. | .. | 5 0 | 5 50 | .. | .. | 8 5 | 8 15 | 9 43 | .. | .. |
| 65½ | Charlton Kings | .. | .. | 8 36 | .. | 10 48 | .. | 1 0 | .. | 2 21 | .. | .. | 5 8 | 5 58 | .. | .. | .. | 8K21 | 9 50 | .. | .. |
| 66½ | Cheltenham (South) B | .. | .. | 8 39 | .. | 10 52 | .. | 1 3 | .. | 2 24 | .. | .. | 5 12 | 6 0 | .. | .. | 8 14 | 8 24 | 9 55 | .. | .. |
| 68½ | Cheltenham Spa A arr | .. | .. | .. | .. | 10 57 | .. | .. | 1 30 | .. | .. | .. | 5 16 | .. | .. | .. | 8 20 | .. | .. | .. | .. |

Bradshaw's timetable for July 1950.

from Weyhill to Red Post Junction and the laying of a connection there with the main line of the Southern Railway have already been mentioned; these works were brought into use on 5th September, 1943. The capacity of the line was further improved by lengthened crossing loops north of Marlborough to take freight trains of up to 60 wagons, and by alterations in the signalling and layout at Swindon Town 'B' box to permit two-way working over an additional road for a short distance south of the station.

At Chiseldon, a long siding that had hitherto extended southwards from the up loop was connected to the adjacent running line in order to form an additional running loop, and a rearrangement of the signalling enabled the down main line to be used for bi-directional working.

As a result of these (and other) improvements, the former Midland & South Western Junction line emerged from the 1939−45 war as a well-equipped north-to-south cross country route — though it was perhaps ironic that these belated improvements came at a time when road transport was poised to do irreparable harm to the railway industry.

### The British Railways Era

On 1st January, 1948 the line passed into public ownership under the British Transport Commission. For nearly eight years from 2nd April, 1950 it was divided for staff and maintenance purposes between the Western and Southern Regions of British Railways, the boundary point lying immediately north of Grafton station. Upper-quadrant signals and other distinctive Southern Region features made their appearance at various places between Red Post Junction and Grafton, though this stretch reverted to the Western Region on 1st February, 1958. Meanwhile, Southern Region 2−6−0s from Eastleigh had taken over some of the locomotive duties, and these engines continued to work right through from Southampton to Cheltenham and back on certain services.

For locomotive enthusiasts the use of both SR and Western Region motive power ensured that, despite an underlying feeling of ineluctable decline, the Midland & South Western Junction route remained a focus of interest and attention. Locomotives seen on the route in the 1950s included SR 'U' class moguls Nos. 31629, 31639, 31791 and 31808, together with ex-GWR '43XX' 2−6−0s Nos. 6320, 6334 and 6372. Other Great Western classes remained hard at work, and in these last years of passenger operation lineside observers could see '55XX' prairie tanks, '57XX' pannier tanks and 'Manor' class 4−6−0s such as No. 7808 Cookham Manor, No. 7810 Draycott Manor, and No. 7824 Iford Manor.

British Railways standard classes worked over the line on both passenger and freight duties; on 24th April, 1958, for instance, class '4MT' 4−6−0 No. 76065 was noted passing through South Cerney with a down freight, while on 12th May, 1961 No. 75002 was seen at Cheltenham on a M&SWJ passenger working. A summary of some of the locomotive classes seen on the Midland & South Western route after 1923 is given in Table Two, and for the benefit of potential modellers, typical names/numbers are printed in the right hand column.

## Table Two

*PRINCIPAL LOCOMOTIVE CLASSES USED ON THE M&SWJ 1923–61*

| Type | Wheelbase | Typical Numbers |
|---|---|---|
| 3521 class | 4–4–0 | 3553 |
| Duke class | 4–4–0 | 3273 *Mounts Bay*/3278 *Trefusis* |
| 43XX class | 2–6–0 | 4381/5306/5322/5371/6320/6334/6387/6372/6395 |
| 45XX class | 2–6–2T | 4538/4551/4585/5510 |
| Dean Goods | 0–6–0 | |
| 2251 class | 0–6–0 | |
| 57XX class | 0–6–0PT | 9600 |
| Manor class | 4–6–0 | 7808 *Cookham Manor*/7810 *Draycott Manor*/7824 *Iford Manor* |
| 51XX class | 2–6–2T | |
| U class | 2–6–0 | 31629/31639/31791/31808 |
| Standard 4MT | 4–6–0 | 75002/76065/76028 |

## Rundown and Closure

The 1950s were a time of retraction for rural lines throughout the British Isles, and with the government of the day making no secret of its dislike for the nationalised railways, it was inevitable that the Midland & South Western Junction route would become a candidate for closure.

First signs of an imminent rundown came in the mid-1950s, when the branch passenger service between Ludgershall and Tidworth was withdrawn after the last train on 17th September, 1955. The working of the Tidworth branch passed into the hands of the War Department on 28th November, 1955, and thereafter the line remained in operation for goods and military traffic.

The decline in the fortunes of the M&SWJ line reached ever lower levels, until on 30th June, 1958 reductions in the passenger service left only one through train each way on weekdays between Cheltenham and Andover, with a further two between Swindon and Andover. The link with the former Midland Railway at Cheltenham was severed on 3rd November, 1958, when the surviving through train to and from Andover was diverted to Cheltenham (St. James) station.

The future of the Midland & South Western Junction route at a time of rising costs and road competition was dark indeed, and local enthusiasts feared that their railway was soon to be axed in its entirety. Meanwhile, on and from 15th September, 1958 all traffic between Marlborough Low Level and Grafton was diverted to run via Savernake (Low Level), and the High Level station was closed, ostensibly as a temporary measure pending repairs to weak underline bridges across the Kennet and Avon Canal and Great Western main line near Wolfhall Junction. In the event this closure turned out to be permanent, and by April 1960 the track had been lifted from Wolfhall Junction to a point just north of Savernake (High Level) station.

General closure followed in 1961, and it was announced that passenger services between Cheltenham and Southampton via Marlborough and

Andover would cease on and from Monday, 11th September. The last trains ran on the preceding Sunday, the very last passenger working being the 8.35 pm from Andover to Swindon, which was headed by '43XX' 2−6−0 No. 6395. A wreath was placed on the front of the locomotive, and the train left Andover accompanied by a barrage of detonators. The closure was marked by the running of two enthusiast specials, one of which was hauled by 'Manor' class 4−6−0 No. 7808 *Cookham Manor* while the other was headed by '43XX' class 2−6−0 No. 5306.

The September 1961 closure left isolated sections of line in operation for goods traffic, namely, Andover Junction to Ludgershall, and from Swindon Town to Cirencester. In addition, the line between Savernake (Low Level) and Marlborough, the southern two miles of which had formed part of the Marlborough Branch of the former Great Western Railway, was kept open for goods traffic until 19th May, 1964, and thereafter for coal only until Marlborough coal yard was finally closed on 7th September, 1964.

Other goods services were also rather shortlived. Facilities were withdrawn from Cricklade and South Cerney on 1st July, 1963, from Cirencester (Watermoor) on 1st April, 1964, and from Swindon Town on 19th May, 1964 for general goods, although the last-named continued to handle coal traffic until 1st November, 1966. Ludgershall remained open for public goods traffic until 24th March, 1969, and still deals with military traffic conveyed over the 7 miles of line from Andover worked as a private siding.

In the Swindon area, the section from Rushey Platt Junction to Swindon Town, and to Moredon power station was worked as a siding from 14th June, 1965. Its subsequent fortunes can be briefly told. After the closure of Swindon Town coal yard on 1st November, 1966, oil tanks were conveyed on a private siding basis to the Esso depot in Marlborough Road, Swindon for the next two years. This was followed by a burst of activity in the latter part of 1970 when many trainloads of roadstone were transferred into road vehicles in the former goods yard for use on the M4 motorway. At that time the old M&SWJ engine shed still survived by the side of Marlborough Road, but it was subsequently demolished to make way for a new road layout.

The fate of the northern arm from Rushey Platt to Moredon remained in the balance. Moredon power station was taken out of commission in 1973 for conversion to oil-firing, thus bringing to an end the coal traffic from Rushey Platt. It seemed possible that, when the power station was recommissioned, oil would be brought in by rail, but not necessarily via Rushey Platt Junction as the construction of a loop from the Gloucester line to the M&SWJ was under consideration. Such a loop would enable the M&SWJ line south of the new connection to be closed, and in the event the latter course of action was decided upon; the demolition of a stone arched bridge that had carried the Midland & South Western Junction line over the busy A420 Oxford to Chippenham trunk road took place on Sunday, 7th September, 1980, and the M&SWJ route was thereby severed for good.

There had in the meantime been a suggestion that the line between Swindon & Cricklade could be operated as a preserved railway, and in February 1978 a public meeting was held with the aim of forming a preservation group for the Swindon to Cricklade line. From these small beginnings grew the Swindon & Cricklade Railway Society, which soon established itself on the site of Blunsdon station, to the north of Swindon.

In February 1983 the society took delivery of its first working steam engine when Andrew Barclay 0–4–0ST *Richard Trevithick* arrived at Blunsdon; this oil-burning industrial locomotive had been purchased from the Swanage Railway by a S & C society member. By 1985 the society's collection of locomotives and rolling stock had increased to six steam and four diesel engines, together with eight passenger vehicles. Half a mile of former M&SWJ line was in operation at weekends and on bank holidays.

### Postscript — The Railway Today

The physical remains of the Midland & South Western Junction line present the appearance of most other closed railways. The majority of the bridges have been dismantled, and although it is possible to follow the course of the railway for many miles, it has vanished without trace and beyond recovery in some places. Flooded gravel pits encroach upon the line near South Cerney, the M4 motorway and other road works have swept it away south of Swindon, and at Ogbourne part of the by-pass is laid upon its course.

At Cirencester, the attractive stone station buildings have been demolished, and a roundabout now occupies the site, but elsewhere one or two of the other M&SWJ stations survive as private dwellings, in particular at Grafton — a most pleasing conversion that retains the awning over the southbound platform. At Savernake the Low Level station on the GWR main line was cleared away completely in September 1968, but meanwhile its one-time rival on the high level had been converted into a cottage-type residence in a setting that has kept platforms, station buildings, water tower and signal box grouped together in a recognisable station ensemble. Viewed at a distance across the fields it is thus possible to get a remarkably vivid reminder of the M&SWJ station at Savernake as it existed over fifty years ago.

In conclusion, it is worth reflecting that, even in its palmiest days, the Midland & South Western Junction Railway as a commercial venture never truly paid. However enterprising the management and train services, however colourful to onlookers its trains and engines, however magnificent its wartime efforts, for most of those who had found the capital for its construction it had been a disastrous investment. The shareholders of the neighbouring Didcot, Newbury & Southampton Railway suffered much the same misfortunes, and it is ironic that both these railways, which proved so valuable to the whole community in time of war, should in fact have been built at the personal cost and sacrifice of a comparatively few private individuals.

Yet the dismal years of bankruptcy and neglect were surely lost to sight in the brilliance of later achievements. The Midland & South Western Junction Railway earned in its day the pride and affection of all right-thinking Wiltshiremen as being in its origin something of a native enterprise — and the only railway to plunge boldly north and south across the grain of that delightful county. In Gloucestershire too there was affection for the M&SWJ,

and elderly residents still recall the smart red trains that were, in many ways, superior to their Great Western counterparts. Today, the abandoned earthworks that once carried the Midland & South Western Junction Railway through three counties stand as lonely and deserted as any pre-historic trackway, and one can feel only sadness that the railway is no more.

# Sources

Primary sources for this history of the M&SWJR included Acts of Parliament, company minute books, correspondence, local newspapers and other contemporary material, but there are in addition several books or articles that may be of interest to those seeking further information including the following:

H. Grote Lewin, *The Railway Mania & Its Aftermath 1845–52* (1936)
E. T. MacDermot, *The History of the Great Western Railway* (1927)
A. G. Bradley and others, *History of Marlborough College* (1923)
C. F. Dendy Marshall, *A History of the Southern Railway* (1936)
Clement E. Stretton, *The History of the Midland Railway* (1901)
E. A. Pratt, *British Railways & the Great War* (1921)
E. L. Ahrons, *Locomotive & Train Working in the Latter Part of the Nine-teenth Century* (1953)
*The Railway Magazine*, especially Volume Four (1899) p. 321 (P. A. Lush-ington) and Volume Seventy (1932) pp. 157 & 255 (D. S. Barrie)
*The Locomotive*, especially Volume Five (1900) pp. 56, 70, 89, 102 & 121 (articles by F. S. Hollansche)
*The Great Western Railway Magazine*, Volume Thirty Five (1923) p. 493, *The Times*, *The Illustrated London News*, *The Engineer*, *The Railway Times*, *Herapath's Journal*, *The Railway Gazette*, *Bradshaw's Guide*, *Bradshaw's Railway Manual*, *The Andover Standard*, *The Cheltenham Examiner*, *The Marlborough Times*, *The North Wilts Herald*, *The Southampton Times*, *The Wilts & Gloucester Standard*

Midland and South Western Junction Railway.
(170)                                                                    [W. & S. Ltd.]

TO

# WITHINGTON

# Supplementary Bibliography

N. Hawkins & R. Murman, Marlborough M&SWJR, *Railway Modeller*, February 1981

T. A. Lindsay, Midland & South Western Junction Railway 0−6−0T, *Model Railway News*, April 1962

Brian Huxley, Jinty at the Junction (M&SWJ 0−4−4T No. 15), *Railway Modeller*, January 1978

C. J. Freezer, Two Foreigners (M&SWJ 2−4−0s), *Railway Modeller*, May 1968

T. A. Lindsay, Midland & South Western Junction Railway 2−4−0, *Model Railway News*, March 1963

W. Hardin Osborne, Midland & South Western Junction Railway 4−4−4T, *Railway Modeller*, March 1966

C. Hamilton Ellis, The North Express, *Railway Magazine*, January 1983

Ken Werrett, Midland & South Western Junction Railway 10 ton Goods Van, *Railway Modeller*, June 1975

Ken Werrett, Midland & South Western Junction Railway 10 ton Bolster Wagon, *Railway Modeller*, December 1976

Ken Werrett, Midland & South Western Junction Railway 10 ton Flat Wagon, *Railway Modeller*, April 1977

Ken Werrett, Midland & South Western Junction Railway Dumb Buffered Bolster Wagon, *Railway Modeller*, July 1977

David Bartholomew *The Midland & South Western Junction Railway* (1982)

# Acknowledgments (to First Edition)

The author is greatly indebted to the Archivist of the British Transport Commission and his staff for their readiness in making available numerous files of correspondence, minute books, reports of Parliamentary proceedings, and other material relating to the line.

Grateful acknowledgment for assistance is due also to the Public Relations and Publicity Officer of British Railways, Western Region, the Curator (Historical Relics), British Transport Commission, the Chief Inspecting Officer of Railways, Ministry of Transport, the Librarian, Ministry of Transport, the Honorary Librarian of the Railway Club, the Earl of Cardigan (for access to the Savernake Estate records), D. S. Barrie, C. R. Clinker, F. K. Davies, J. L. Farmer, the Rev. J. C. Gibson, M. D. Greville, R. W. Kidner, T. S. Lascelles, E. R. Mountford, G. A. Newman, P. J. T. Reed and R. C. Riley. Thanks are especially due to R. M. Robbins for his suggestions and for editing the manuscript.

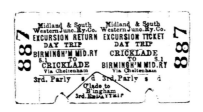

A '43XX' class No. 6320 seen here waiting at Tidworth with a two coach local service. The station buildings here were of the standard MSWJ design.                H.C. Casserley

MSWJR 4–4–0 No. 2 (seen here as GWR No. 1120) at Swindon works on the 11th September, 1927. The engine was at that time still in MSWJ red livery.

H.C. Casserley

# Index